P9-CAF-829

DISCARD

CENTRALIA HIGH SCHOOL LIBRARY
CENTRALIA, WASHINGTON 98531

T 37706

The POWER Series

CARRIER BATTLE GROUP

S. F. Tomajczyk

MBI Publishing Company

Dedicated to my Navy Heroes:
CDR Charles F. Tomajczyk, Jr. USN (Ret.)
Capt. E Ross Mintz, USN (Deceased)

First published in 2000 by MBI Publishing Company, 729 Prospect Avenue, PO Box 1, Osceola, WI 54020-0001 USA

© S. F. Tomajczyk, 2000

All rights reserved. With the exception of quoting brief passages for the purposes of review no part of this publication may be reproduced without prior written permission from the Publisher.

The information in this book is true and complete to the best of our knowledge. All recommendations are made without any guarantee on the part of the author or Publisher, who also disclaim any liability incurred in connection with the use of this data or specific details.

We recognize that some words, model names and designations, for example, mentioned herein are the property of the trademark holder. We use them for identification purposes only. This is not an official publication.

MBI Publishing Company books are also available at discounts in bulk quantity for industrial or sales-promotional use. For details write to Special Sales Manager at Motorbooks International Wholesalers & Distributors, 729 Prospect Avenue, PO Box 1, Osceola, WI 54020-0001 USA.

Library of Congress Cataloging-in-Publication Data Available

ISBN: 0-7603-0707-5

On the front cover: Displacing some 97,000 tons with its combat load, the USS *George Washington* (CVN-73) plows through the high seas during a recent six-month deployment. *U.S. Navy*

On the frontispiece: Just a few of the combatants in a typical carrier battle group, seen here steaming in close proximity for a publicity shot. When further out to sea, the group will disperse into a formation covering more than 100 miles, with ships keeping stations suitable for its mission. *U.S. Navy*

On the title page: The amphibious assault ship USS *Bataan* (LHD-5) as it patrols the fictitious Gulf of Sabani during JTFEX 99-2. *S. F. Tomajczyk*

On the back cover: Three Arleigh Burke–class destroyers, the *Higgins* (DDG-76), *Donald Cook* (DDG-75), and USS *Mahan* (DDG-72), at sea in late 1998. *Bath Iron Works*

Edited by Mike Haenggi
Designed by Bruce Leckie

Printed in China

Table of Contents

"What the hell is that?" I asked myself. "A sandbar?" I peered through the round, hand-sized window—one of only two on the C-2 Greyhound—at the ocean far below. It was late June, and I was flying out to the USS *George Washington* (CVN-73) where I was scheduled to spend time watching carrier operations and to interview the carrier's senior officers. So far it had been an uneventful and noisy flight, even though I had my earplugs and cranial headphones in place. A heavy fog, created by the cool, air-conditioned air mixing with the moist, tropical air, swirled about me in the cabin. I distinctly felt as if I was in a Halloween horror movie.

I wiped the condensation from the window and searched the ocean again. Sure enough, a white, horizontal streak could clearly be seen on the surface. Odd, I had never seen waves breaking on a sandbar so far out to sea before. As I pondered the sight, the Greyhound banked to the left and suddenly . . . there IT was: the *George Washington*.

It was huge, filling the entire window. I felt foolish as a wave of revelation washed over me. What I had seen was *not* a sandbar but the wake of the aircraft carrier as it sliced neatly through the sea at 30 knots. How could I have been so stupid? After all, my father had been a naval officer and I had seen numerous aircraft carriers in my life.

I glanced to my left and was immediately relieved that the lieutenant commander seated next to me didn't seem to notice my embarrassment.

"That's the GW," he yelled. "Keep looking. There's more."

I nodded and turned back to the window. A few minutes later a Ticonderoga-class cruiser came into sight, followed several minutes later by a Spruance-class destroyer. Out on the horizon, I could make out the silhouette of an amphibious assault ship.

"That's only a small part of a battle group," the lieutenant commander said loudly. "I don't know how you're going to be able to write about it. It's too big for a book. It's what the Navy is all about."

A knot formed in my stomach as I began to realize the immensity of the project I was embarking on. The lieutenant commander was right: An aircraft carrier battle group is huge, embracing 10 warships, 2 nuclear attack submarines, 1 replenishment ship, 2,200 Marines, 13,000-plus sailors, and an air wing of 70 aircraft. On top of this, the battle group is capable of waging war in a number of different and unique arenas, including electronic warfare, antisubmarine warfare, anti-air warfare, surface warfare, amphibious assault, air strikes, combat air patrols, and reconnaissance.

Who was I kidding? How do you condense all this into a 128-page book, especially when an entire book could be written (and may have!) on each of these topics?

Quite simply, you do the best you can, realizing that even most naval officers do not fully comprehend what a battle group can do. All they know is that it is huge. It is powerful. It inspires humility and, in the eyes of the enemy, trepidation. That is what I have tried to capture in this book.

I extend my heartfelt thanks to the following individuals and Navy and Marine Corps commands for their assistance in making this book a reality, especially given the tight time constraints we were all subject to: Diane Palermo, Naval Surface Warfare Center; Lieutenant Commander Mark McCaffrey, COMSUBLANT; Lieutenant Commander Bob Ross, PAO, SUBGRUTWO; Commander James P. Ransom III, CO, USS *Miami* (SSN-755); Lieutenant Commander Chris Williams, XO, USS *Miami* (SSN-755); Lieutenant

Commander Carl Lahti, navigator, USS *Miami* (SSN-755); Commander Roxie T. Merritt, PAO, COMNAVAIRLANT; Mike Maus, public affairs specialist, COMNAVAIRLANT; Barry Higginbotham, deputy for media, CINCLANTFLT; JO1 Michael J. Viola, staff journalist, CINCLANTFLT; JOC David Rourk, media action officer, CINCLANTFLT; Lieutenant Commander Ron Hill, PAO, NAVSPECWARGRUT-WO; OSCM(SW) Delta Hinson, NAVPHIBASE Little Creek; Captain David M. Griesmer, USMC, USACOM Public Affairs Office; Colonel Walter E. Gaskin, USMC, CO, 22d MEU (SOC); Lieutenant Colonel Jerome M. Lynes, USMC, operations officer, 22d MEU (SOC); Captain Mark A. S. Oswell, USMC, PAO, 22d MEU (SOC); Rear Admiral J. Michael Johnson, commander, CARGRUSIX; Vice Admiral William Fallon, Second Fleet; Captain Stephen C. Jasper, commodore, Amphibious Squadron Six; Captain D. C. Taylor, CO, USS *Bataan* (LHD-5); Major Kirk Barley, USMC, operations officer, USS *Bataan* (LHD-5); Captain Robin Weber, CO, USS *John F. Kennedy* (CV-67); Captain Michael Wanjon, XO, USS *John F. Kennedy* (CV-67); Lieutenant Joe Walker, PAO, USS *John F. Kennedy* (CV-67); JOC (SW/AW) Michael Hart, PA assistant, USS *John F. Kennedy* (CV-67); ABFC (AW) Kevin Sayre, Flight Deck CPO, USS *John F. Kennedy* (CV-67); Captain Craig T. Cunninghame, CAG, Carrier Air Wing One; Captain William D. Crowder, commander, Destroyer Squadron 24; Captain L. G. "Yank" Rutherford, CO, USS *George Washington* (CVN-73); Lieutenant Herb Josey, PAO, USS *George Washington* (CVN-73); RMC (AW) Joe Reinish, USS *George Washington* (CVN-73); Captain Schapman, CO, USS Nassau (LHA-4); Captain Gerry Maver, XO, USS Nassau (LHA-4); Commander Tim Alexander, Air Boss, USS *Nassau* (LHA-4); Lieutenant Mike Patterson, mini boss, USS *Nassau* (LHA-4); Lieutenant Chris W. Brunett, flight deck officer, USS *Nassau* (LHA-4); JO1 Mike Raney, PA assistant, USS *Nassau* (LHA-4); Commander Roger Coldiron, CO, USS *Stump* (DD-978); Captain Denis V. Army, CO, USS *Cape St. George* (CG-71); Lieutenant Commander Mark Sedlacek, XO, USS *Cape St. George* (CG-71); Lieutenant Pat Brophy, air warfare officer, USS *Cape St. George* (CG-71); Troy R. Snead, PAO, NAS Oceana; Commander Mark "Shaker" Adamshick, CO, VF-213; Lieutenant Commander Bob "Jumby" Castleton, VF-213; Lieutenant Joe "Snacker" Dalton, VF-213; Lieutenant (jg) Brian "Beke" Hodges, VF-213; Lieutenant (jg) Kevin Watkins, VF-213; Christopher J. Madden, director, *Navy News* photo; Lieutenant Rick Naystatt, deputy director, *Navy News* photo; Cora L. Fields, public affairs officer, NAS Point Mugu; Christopher P. Cavas, news editor, *Navy Times;* Michael J. Tull, senior manager/communications, Military Aircraft and Missile Systems Group, the Boeing Company; Dina Weiss, the Boeing Company; Rusty Robertson, public affairs, Bath Iron Works; Cindy Coffee, Teledyne Ryan Aeronautics; Rear Admiral Thomas J. Cassidy Jr. (USN, retired), CEO, General Atomics Aeronautical Systems Inc.; Rebe Philip, marketing assistant, General Atomics Aeronautical Systems Inc.; James Raylor, project manager (UAV), General Atomics Aeronautical Systems Inc.; Naval Sea Systems Command (David Caskey, Dick Cole, and Patricia Dolan); and the Navy's Office of Information (Lieutenant Robert Mehal and Lieutenant Patrick J. Moore).

I also want to thank the pilots and crews of VRC-40 Rawhides for flying me safely aboard the aircraft carriers at sea (Love those Gs! Find my eyeballs yet?), and to the crews of the following ships for the hospitality and assistance they provided me during my visits: USS *Miami* (SSN-755); USS *Stump* (DD-978); USS *Cape St. George* (CG-71); USS *Nassau* (LHA-4); USS *George Washington* (CVN-73); USS *John F. Kennedy* (CV-67); USS *Bataan* (LHD-5); and LCAC-84 of Assault Craft Unit 4.

Chapter 1

Battle Group Power
Immense in Scope

CARRIER BATTLE GROUP. Say it aloud three times and you will begin to see Darth Vader-like images in your head. It is a phrase that reeks of power and destruction. And that is because, quite simply, an aircraft carrier battle group (CVBG) is indeed powerful and destructive. Made up of some dozen warships—cruisers, destroyers, and nuclear attack submarines—a battle group can successfully wage war against anyone, anywhere in the world.

When you stand on the flight deck of an aircraft carrier—or as sailors like to say, "up on the roof"—you are impressed with its immense size, which encompasses some 4 1/2 acres of steel and tarmac. But that is the aircraft carrier alone, just one vessel of the battle group. You must look out to sea to find the other warships to better understand what a battle group truly looks like. When you do, you will likely see only one other vessel anywhere near you—a destroyer or cruiser that serves in the "Redcrown" role. It is responsible for constantly monitoring the airspace over the entire CVBG for any signs of an incoming cruise missile or enemy fighter aircraft. That's it. The rest of the ocean—all the way out to the horizon, and all around you—is empty. That's because the remaining warships of the battle group are deployed as far

> *There is no weapon platform or system that is as valuable to (America) as the large-deck aircraft carrier.*
>
> **Representative Herb Bateman (R-Virginia) Chairman, House Armed Services Committee's Readiness Subcommittee**

away as 60 to 100 miles from the aircraft carrier, covering all points of the compass.

Although an aircraft carrier is impressive in size, the area that a battle group physically occupies—thousands of square nautical miles—is imposing. Even more mind-boggling is the amount of sea and air space that a CVBG actively controls when deployed. As one tactical action officer (TAO) aboard the USS *George Washington* (CVN-73) bluntly put it, "If you put our battle group on land in the Midwest, everything from the Gulf coast of Texas to Lake Michigan would be in our sphere of control."

This point is reinforced by Rear Admiral (Select) Lindell G. "Yank" Rutherford, commanding officer of the *Washington,* who says, "I could comfortably and successfully launch an attack against New York City from Virginia Beach."

So when you hear the words *carrier battle group,* it is understandable why you are unable to visualize it in your head. First, it is simply too large to grasp. Second, the collective firepower and the special capabilities represented by the battle group are beyond comprehension. That is why this book exists. Its purpose is to help you digest the awesome power represented by an aircraft carrier battle group, the most lethal military force ever assembled in the history of

What a real carrier battle group looks like at sea. This aerial view of the conventionally powered USS *John F. Kennedy* (CV-67) was taken from a CH-46 Sea Knight helicopter during the July 1999 joint task force exercise. The other eight surface ships of the battle group are located up to 50 miles away. If you have ever wondered why the carrier island is placed on the right side of the flight deck, it is because studies conducted since the 1920s have shown that pilots instinctively tend to turn to the left when landing. So the placement of the island was done to minimize the risk of a collision. *S. F. Tomajczyk*

Rear Admiral John M. "Carlos" Johnson is the commander of the USS *John F. Kennedy* battle group, which is designated as Carrier Group Six (CARGRUSIX). This photo was taken of the admiral as he watched launch and recovery operations from the *Kennedy's* Flag Bridge. As the battle group commander, he has a host of Navy captains and commanders within the CVBG who report to him, each responsible for a particular combat mission. For instance, the commanding officer of a guided-missile cruiser or destroyer may be tasked with protecting the battle group from aerial attack (known as the "Redcrown" role), while another CO may be responsible for antisubmarine operations. *S. F. Tomajczyk*

the world. The book accomplishes this by delving into the four spheres a CVBG is simultaneously exposed to and involved in: antisubmarine warfare, air warfare, surface warfare, and electronic warfare.

Before that is done, however, it is helpful to have an understanding of how carrier battle groups have evolved over the decades, how modern battle groups are composed, and what trends are influencing the capabilities of a battle group.

The Early Years

In the beginning, there was the battleship. Displacing some 50,000 tons fully loaded, it bristled bow-to-stern with dozens of heavy guns and could steam like an Olympic sprinter at 30 knots. The battleship was truly the rabid dog of the high seas, capable of intimidating any naval fleet it encountered.

That all changed, however, on June 3 to 6, 1942, when Japanese and U.S. forces collided in the South Pacific near a circular-shaped, 6-mile-diameter atoll known as Midway Island. The event was the turning point in military history where battleships and aircraft carriers were concerned. It was during the Battle of Midway that the grande dame of naval warfare—the battleship—went the way of the dinosaur. Fought some 1,150 miles west-northwest of Hawaii, this engagement marked the first time that two naval forces battled one another without their warships ever coming within sight of each other. The combat itself was exclusively fought by aircraft: propeller-driven fighters and bombers dueling it out over the Pacific Ocean.

The event sealed forever the carrier's future as the centerpiece of naval battle groups. It showed that a nation could project overwhelming military force through aircraft deployed by a ship. While a battleship's so-called "death zone" was limited to about 23 miles—the reach of its 16-inch guns—an aircraft carrier's lethal power was restricted only by the range of its fighters and bombers, which continued to increase with each subsequent generation of aircraft design. Hence, the United States quickly reshuffled its military force, placing the aircraft carrier as the Queen of the battle group, with frigates, cruisers, battleships, and destroyers playing a subservient role by protecting the carrier from harm.

In the years following World War II, which were marked by the advent of jet aircraft, the proliferation of nuclear weapons and the arrival of the Cold War, American military aircraft were redesigned to carry nuclear bombs that originally weighed 12,000 pounds apiece but were soon reduced to under a quarter of that weight. This, in turn, forced the Navy to redesign its aircraft carriers to accommodate those aircraft. Carriers not only increased in size—nearly doubling from 42,113 tons (USS *Lexington*) in 1941 to 79,250 tons (*Forrestal*) in 1952—but they also introduced angled flight decks, automated approach and landing aids, and steam-powered catapult systems to rapidly launch a large number of aircraft from an armored flight deck. Further improvements, such as placing elevators on the edge of the flight deck, increased the size of the flat-top area while keeping it relatively uncluttered. Nuclear reactors also showed up, allowing the Navy to keep a forward presence anywhere in the world without having to worry about running out of fuel.

In the 1960s, a stand-off attack capability was given to the carrier battle group with the creation of the Harpoon antiship missile. This development, as well as the introduction of the Tomahawk cruise missile in the 1980s, significantly expanded the death zone around a CVBG. A battle group could now accurately attack enemy targets located well over the horizon: The AGM-84 Harpoon could sink ships at distances of 80-plus miles, and the BGM-109 Tomahawk (T-LAM variant) could hit land targets 610 miles away.

In 1983, a battle group's air combat capability was significantly enhanced with the arrival of AEGIS, an integrated system of sophisticated sensors that enables a warship to track 128 targets simultaneously. Placed aboard a battle group's guided missile cruisers and destroyers, AEGIS allows these ships to detect incoming missiles and aircraft and quickly launch missiles against them.

The most recent noteworthy advancement to a battle group's power occurred in 1991 when the Arleigh Burke–class of guided missile destroyer was commissioned. In addition to it possessing the AEGIS system, the *Arleigh Burke* was the first Navy ship designed with special hatches and an overpressure system, which enable it to fight in nuclear, biological, or chemical environments. This means a battle group can continue to show a presence and fight even if weapons of mass destruction (WMD) are used. In the past, a CVBG would have had to leave a contaminated area, opening the possibility that the enemy would capitalize on its absence.

A Modern Battle Group

Today, the United States has 13 aircraft carriers in service. A battle group can be formed around each of these. These carriers are assigned to one of two major naval operating forces, as shown in the sidebar "America's Aircraft Carriers" on page 12. The largest carriers are those of the Nimitz-class (CVN 68-76), some of which can displace more than 102,000 tons when fully loaded. The last ship of this class, the *Ronald Reagan,* is currently under construction at Newport News Shipbuilding in Virginia. It is scheduled to replace the USS *Constellation,* which will be 41 years old when the *Reagan* is delivered to the Navy in 2002.

There is another carrier under construction right now at Newport News. Known simply as the CVN-77 (a name has not yet been selected), it will eventually replace the *Kitty Hawk,* which will be 47 when it is retired in 2008. The CVN-77 is going to be the sole ship in its own class, for it is considered by the Navy to be a transition aircraft carrier, intended to introduce a plethora of new technologies and stealth designs in preparation for the next major class of carrier, the CVX (aircraft carrier, experimental). The CVX, if funded, will begin entering service with the Navy around 2013 and will incorporate many of the

A port-quarter view of the USS *Theodore Roosevelt* (CVN-71) as it lies at anchor off Nassau, Bahamas. Vertically, the ship is 244 feet tall from the tip of its island structure to the ocean's surface—the same as a 24-story building. *U.S. Navy*

This chart provides the name, hull number, and homeport for each of the 13 aircraft carriers currently in service with the Navy.

The U.S. Pacific Fleet provides warships for the Seventh Fleet (which operates in the Indian Ocean and western Pacific) and the Third Fleet (which operates in the eastern and northern Pacific). The Fifth Fleet is also assigned to USPACFLT, but it only exists in times of crisis or war. Pacific Fleet battle groups and task forces have the distinction of operating in the "mother of all maritime theaters"—102 million square miles of ocean representing 52 percent of the Earth's ocean area.

As a result of the Department of the Navy's downsizing and reorganization efforts, San Diego may eventually become the homeport of three nuclear flattops (after the *Constellation* is decommissioned)—the *Stennis, Nimitz,* and *Reagan*. Navy proposals would keep the carriers *Lincoln* and *Vinson* in Washington state. No carrier would be based at Pearl Harbor.

The U.S. Atlantic Fleet provides naval forces for the Second Fleet (which operates in the Atlantic and the

Caribbean and Barents seas) and the Sixth Fleet (which operates in the Mediterranean Sea). It is important to note that the *Kennedy* is considered to be a reserve carrier. It assists in the ongoing training of naval aviators, enabling them to practice launch and recovery procedures. The *Kennedy* has retained its weapon systems, however, and can be deployed overseas if an international crisis or war flares up.

U.S. Pacific Fleet (USPACFLT)
Nimitz Class
USS *Carl Vinson* (CVN-70), Bremerton, Washington
USS *Abraham Lincoln* (CVN-72), Everett, Washington
USS *John C. Stennis* (CVN-74), San Diego, California
Ronald Reagan (CVN-76), San Diego, California—Under construction

Other
USS *Kitty Hawk* (CV-63), Yokosuka, Japan—(Nickname: Kitty)
USS *Constellation* (CV-64), San Diego, California—(Nickname: Connie)

U.S. Atlantic Fleet (USLANTFLT)
Nimitz Class
USS *Nimitz* (CVN-68), Newport News, Virginia
USS *Dwight D. Eisenhower* (CVN-69), Norfolk, Virginia (Nickname: Ike)
USS *Theodore Roosevelt* (CVN-71), Norfolk, Virginia (Nicknames: TR and Teddy)
USS *George Washington* (CVN-73), Norfolk, Virginia (Nickname: GW)
USS *Harry S. Truman* (CVN-75), Norfolk, Virginia

Other
USS *Enterprise* (CVN-65), Norfolk, Virginia (Nickname: *Big E*)
USS *John F. Kennedy* (CV-67), Mayport, Florida (Nickname: *Big John*)

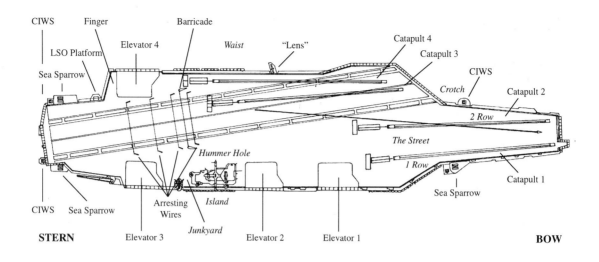

CIWS   Finger   Barricade

LSO Platform   Elevator 4   *Waist*   "Lens"   Catapult 4

Sea Sparrow   Catapult 3

CIWS

Crotch

Catapult 2

2 Row

The Street

1 Row

Catapult 1

Sea Sparrow

Hummer Hole

CIWS   Sea Sparrow   Arresting Wires   *Island*

STERN   Elevator 3   *Junkyard*   Elevator 2   Elevator 1   **BOW**

Layout of a Nimitz-Class
Aircraft Carrier (CVN-68)

features proven aboard the CVN-77 in addition to any new high-tech developments, such as an electromagnetic catapult, antiship laser weapons, or robotic servicing equipment on the flight deck.

A typical CVBG is made up of up to a dozen ships, which provide various capabilities in support of battle group operations:

- Two *guided missile cruisers:* These are multimission surface combatants that are equipped with Tomahawk missiles for long-range strike capability. An example of a guided missile cruiser is the *Ticonderoga* class (CG 47-73).
- One *guided missile destroyer:* A multimission surface combatant used mainly for anti-air warfare (AAW). The Arleigh Burke class (DDG 51-88) is the primary class of guided missile destroyers.
- One *destroyer:* A Spruance-class (DD 963-997) surface combatant that assumes the role of anti-submarine warfare (ASW).
- One *frigate:* An Oliver Hazard Perry–class (FFG 7-61) surface combatant that mainly provides anti-submarine warfare capabilities.
- Two *attack submarines:* Nuclear-powered attack submarines of the Los Angeles class (SSN 688-773) destroy hostile surface ships and submarines, conduct reconnaissance missions, insert special operations forces, and launch Tomahawk missiles in support of land strikes. The new Seawolf class (SSN 21-23) of attack submarine has recently joined the CVBG.
- One *replenishment:* A combined ammunition, oiler, and supply ship of either the supply class (AOE 6-10) or Sacramento class (AOE 1-4) provides the CVBG with the food, ammunition, and fuel it needs to remain on station, ready to respond to a crisis.

Based on this description, here is what the *Theodore Roosevelt* battle group looks like (Keep in mind that the aircraft carrier itself is loaded with some 75 aircraft and 5,500 sailors and airmen.):

USS *Roosevelt* (CVN-71)
USS *Leyte Gulf* (CG-55)
USS *Vella Gulf* (CG-72)
USS *Peterson* (DD-969)
USS *Ramage* (DDG-61)
USS *Ross* (DDG-71)
USS *Halyburton* (FFG-40)
USS *Elrod* (FFG-55)
USS *Arctic* (AOE-8)

In addition, the CVBG is accompanied by a three-ship amphibious ready group (ARG):

USS *Kearsarge* (LHD-3)
USS *Ponce* (LPD-15)
USS *Gunston Hall* (LSD-44)

These three vessels carry upward of 2,200 marines (and their equipment) of the 26th Marine Expeditionary Unit, which is rated as special operations capable. That means the Marines have been certified as being able to carry out more than two dozen unconventional warfare mission profiles, including in *extremis* hostage rescue, urban warfare, embassy evacuation, and signals intelligence/electronic warfare.

The MEU is able to sustain itself for 15 days of combat before resupply is necessary. A more indepth look at MEUs and amphibious warfare is provided in chapter 7.

Deployment

The presence of American naval warships just offshore—often within eyesight of coastal cities—is the most effective reminder a potential foe can receive of the United State's determination to keep the peace.

A look at the flight deck of the USS *Kennedy,* facing the waist catapults. In the background, two F-14 Tomcats prepare to be launched from the bow catapults. To the left of the Tomcats are several landing signals officers (LSO) standing on their platform. They help guide aircraft to a safe landing aboard the carrier. In front of the Tomcats, on the flight deck, you have a partial view of catapult number four. The Navy may scrap its massive steam-driven catapults and replace them with a lighter-weight, electromagnetic system aboard the future CVX-class of aircraft carrier. *S. F. Tomajczyk*

One of many artists' renderings of what the new CVN-77 aircraft carrier might look like when it finally appears in 2013. This version shows two smaller islands to reduce the carrier's overall radar cross section, thereby making it less visible to enemy radar. *U.S. Navy*

As America and the rest of the world enter the 21st century, it is apparent to the Navy that it can no longer rely on 50-year-old design concepts when building an aircraft carrier. This is especially true with regard to the development and proliferation of long-range cruise missiles, precision-guided munitions, weapons of mass destruction, and laser weapons. To prepare for and respond to these threats, the Navy has decided to trash the blueprints for its flattops and start all over, redesigning the carrier from the keel up.

The CVN-77 is the first stage of this Herculean effort. Now under construction at Newport News Shipbuilding in Virginia, the CVN-77 is based on a Nimitz-class hull and powerplant up to the main deck level, but from there on up everything else is new. Although the final design has not yet been approved, it is known that the CVN-77 will neither look nor operate like any aircraft carrier before it. Composite radar-absorbent materials and angular planes that are the hallmark of the F-117 Nighthawk and the experimental surface ship *Sea Shadow* will undoubtedly be incorporated into the CVN-77 so that it becomes a Stealth carrier, producing a radar cross section no larger than a frigate. This means that the CVN-77 will not have a traditional-looking conning tower. In fact the flight deck may very well be empty or possess two small towers. Internal aircraft elevators will also enhance the ship's stealth.

The CVN-77 will also implement many of the so-called "Smart Ship" systems that have been tested since 1995 on several surface combatants, such as the *Yorktown* (CG-48), Stout (DDG-55), *Ticonderoga* (CG-47), and the *Rushmore* (LSD-47). The Smart Ship program relies on the integration of computer systems and sensors to reduce the need for manpower while increasing overall ship performance. A semi-automated refueling "pit stop" for aircraft is a good example. It will provide faster, more efficient servicing while requiring fewer people. The same holds true for cargo movement devices and ordnance loading systems.

As for weapon systems, the CVN-77 will be more heavily armed than current Nimitz-class carriers. It will be fitted with the rolling airframe missile (RAM) for point defense against incoming missiles, and it will likely have several eight-cell vertical launch systems (VLS) dotting the edges of the flight deck—all capable of firing Tomahawk cruise missiles and clusters of the forthcoming Evolved Sea Sparrow Missile (ESSM).

And last, the CVN-77 will be capable of rapid reconfiguration. In a world where the Navy increasingly finds itself responding to humanitarian efforts and policing actions, it is prudent to give a carrier some adaptability. For instance, the interior hangars will be reconfigurable to handle a variety of situations, such as housing refugees or storing unmanned aerial vehicles like the Predator.

Additionally, a "Roll-on, Roll-off" (RORO) ramp may be incorporated into the carrier's fantail, allowing vehicles and troops to quickly load and unload from pierside. At sea, the ramp could also serve as a type of "port" for amphibious craft, such as the air-cushioned LCAC and the Navy SEAL rigid-hull inflatable boat (RHIB).

The CVN-77 will be a one-ship class. Its purpose is to test a new generation of advanced warfare technologies. Those systems that prove themselves will eventually find themselves—in an upgraded manner, of course—in the Navy's next major class of aircraft carrier, the CVX, which will appear in 2013.

Three ships of the USS *George Washington* battle group transit the Suez Canal as they head from the Mediterranean Sea to the Persian Gulf. The battle group was ordered to the Persian Gulf to join the aircraft carrier USS *Nimitz* (CVN-68) battle group already on station and enforce the no-fly zone over southern Iraq. The ships in this photo are the USS *Normandy* (CG-60) (right), USS *Annapolis* (SSN-760) (middle), and USS *Seattle* (AOE-3) (left). *U.S. Navy*

The sheer size of the warships and the fighters that constantly buzz around them make an indelible impression on foreign leaders—civilian and military alike—often encouraging them to back off and behave.

In peacetime, the Navy deploys three carriers overseas: one in the Mediterranean Sea (Sixth Fleet), one in the western Pacific Ocean (Seventh Fleet), and one in the Indian Ocean or Persian Gulf (Fifth Fleet). Sometimes a fourth carrier is operating in either the Med or Pacific.

These carriers are backed-up by the other nine carriers assigned to bases in the continental United States, but not all nine are available for sea duty. That's because one or two are in shipyards undergoing nuclear refueling or extensive overhauls, and the remainder are in various stages of operational training and routine, dockside maintenance. If a crisis were to arise, however, at least one carrier on each coast could be dispatched immediately (this is called "surged"), followed three to five days later by another carrier on each coast. An example of surging occurred in late 1990 during Operation Desert Shield. By the time Desert Storm was launched on January 15, 1991, six aircraft carrier battle groups were in place to strike against Saddam Hussein's military forces.

The deployment cycle that each CVBG observes is 18 months long and broken into three distinct 6-month phases:

- *Leave/unit training:* A rest period for the crews of the battle group who have just returned home after being at sea for six months. During this time, sailors take leave time and train to keep current with advancements in their field of specialty and in naval warfare.
- *Workup:* An intense period where sailors and ships of the battle group refresh their combat skills. During this time component forces often participate in joint training exercises that test and hone their abilities at antisubmarine warfare, air combat, electronic warfare, and amphibious assault. Toward the end of the workup phase, the entire battle group is certified for deployment through a series of at-sea tests and exercises.
- *Deployment:* The battle group is ordered overseas for six months to respond to crises that arise and, if necessary, wage war.

When deployed, a CVBG represents the powerful arm of the United States, and government leaders since World War II know this. Whenever a crisis arises, one of the first questions asked by the president, the secretary of defense, and the chairman of the joint chiefs of staff is, "Where are the carriers?"

Depending on how close a carrier battle group is to the scene of the crisis and how it is comprised in the way of surface ships, armament, amphibious forces, and so on determines how the CVBG is used. There are a number of missions that a battle group can perform, the majority of which establish and maintain the control of sea and air space:

Show of force: This mission profile requires that a CVBG apply a measured amount of military force against specific targets. Typically, the intent behind a show of force is to bolster a commitment or threat America has made. By doing so, allies are reassured that America will stick by its promises and foes are reminded that the United States means business. "No" means no. For instance, during Operation Desert Fox (December 16 to 20, 1998), the USS *Enterprise* battle group struck Iraqi military targets with more than 300 Tomahawk land-attack missiles and 691,000 pounds of ordnance. The purpose of the 70-hour assault was to significantly reduce Saddam Hussein's capacity to build weapons of mass destruction.

Maritime interdiction: Warships have routinely been used over the centuries to halt and turn away target vessels from certain ports. In 1994, for instance, the United States and its allies were simultaneously running embargo missions against Iraq, Haiti, and in the Balkans. During Operation Allied Force against Yugoslavia in 1999, maritime blockade was once again effectively used, this time in the Adriatic Sea to prevent Serbian forces from being resupplied.

Maritime escort: Sometimes, high-value commercial vessels (such as oil tankers) have to be escorted through dangerous waters and past hostile shores. A battle group can use its assets, for instance, to detect underwater minefields and hostile surface ships that could sink a tanker. An example of a maritime escort mission occurred in 1988 and 1989 when CVBG surface combatants were used to escort American-flagged, Kuwaiti-owned tankers in the Persian Gulf.

Invasion: Although rare, landing Marines and other combat units ashore to accomplish a mission in the best interest of the United States still occurs from time to time. For example, CVBGs were present in the 1983 invasion of Grenada and the 1994 liberation of Haiti. In both instances, the battle group and its amphibious ready group were the primary units used. This also happened during Operation Allied Force in 1999: Elements of the 26th MEU (SOC) went into Kosovo to become part of the U.S. contingent of NATO's multinational peacekeeping force to ensure the safety of returning ethnic Albanian refugees. The Marines came ashore from the USS *Kearsarge* ARG, which was part of the USS *Roosevelt* battle group.

Power projection: This is an event where military presence and firepower are required for long periods of time to support a national commitment. Typically, these incidents require two or more battle groups to share the burden of extended military operations. Examples of power projection include Operation Desert Storm (1991) and Operation Allied Force (1999). In the latter conflict, according to Rear Admiral Winston Copeland, fighters from Carrier Air Wing Eight (CVW-8) flew 3,100 combat sorties from the USS *Roosevelt* during a nine-week period. Obviously, in power projection events such as this, the trick is to pace the pilots and sailors so they don't suffer battle fatigue and to maintain an adequate supply of bombs, rockets, and missiles for delivery onto enemy targets.

Sprains and Strains

With the variety of missions the United States has for its aircraft carrier battle groups, it is no wonder that CVBGs are frequently called upon by government leaders and the National Command Authority to dissolve tensions and enforce foreign policies. Unfortunately, the Navy has been downsizing since the end of the Cold War. The Navy, which had been rapidly building under President Ronald Reagan to become a 600-ship fleet, dramatically began decommissioning its surface combatants and submarines to become a 305-ship fleet by the year 2003 in accordance with a Quadrennial Defense Review mandate. Unfortunately, while the Navy has been shrinking in size, the demand for its warships has increased.

According to a Congressional Research Service study, U.S. armed forces (including the Navy) were used 16 times under President Reagan, 14 times under President Bush, and—so far—more than 25 times under President Clinton.

A recent study done by the Department of the Navy came to similar conclusions. The report points out that during the Cold War (1946 to 1989), the Navy and Marine Corps responded to some 190 crises, an average of about four per year.

By comparison, between 1990 and 1997, they responded to 75 crises, or more than 10 per year. In other words, *double* the Cold War rate.

With U.S. naval forces increasingly involved in larger missions around the world, there is a growing realization in the Pentagon and on Capitol Hill that the fleet should be increasing in size, not slimming down. Otherwise, the Navy will not have enough ships to respond to future crises. This dilemma became quite apparent during Operation Allied Force in 1999, when the Navy found itself frantically reshuffling its carrier battle groups worldwide to address the situation in Kosovo.

In late March, the USS *Roosevelt* battle group was diverted from the Persian Gulf to the Adriatic Sea to bolster allied aircraft striking at Yugoslavia. In turn, the USS *Kitty Hawk* CVBG was ordered from the Pacific to the Persian Gulf to keep an eye on Saddam Hussein. This left the western Pacific without a carrier, a distressing event in light of the renewed tensions between North Korea and South Korea. To fill in for the missing aircraft carrier, the U.S. Pacific Command placed its fighter and bomber aircraft on alert status.

"If we have another flare-up in the world, then we're short," Admiral Paul Reason, Atlantic fleet commander, warned a Senate subcommittee at the time.

Fortunately, there were no more flare-ups, and the war in Kosovo ended after nine weeks of combat.

Downsizing and high-deployment tempo aside, the Navy is faced with yet another predicament. With the dissolution of the Soviet Union, the United States is no longer confronted with the prospect of a deep ocean, "Blue Water" battle between huge carrier battle groups. Instead, it is faced with fighting small and agile naval forces in the shallow littorals (this is known as "Brown Water") of the world. What's wrong with that? Quite simply, the Navy does not have enough of the right ships for that environment. So CVBGs now find themselves learning to adapt in claustrophobic, shallow regions of ocean where the threat from

During Operation Desert Strike in September 1996, the guided-missile cruiser USS *Shiloh* (CG-67) launches a Tomahawk land-attack cruise missile (TLAM) from its vertical launch tube. The missile is programmed to strike a selected air defense target in Iraq to reduce the risk to U.S. and allied pilots enforcing the no-fly zone. *U.S. Navy*

ultraquiet diesel submarines, underwater mines, land-launched missiles, and terrorist groups armed with weapons of mass destruction are ever present.

The beginning of the twenty-first century finds the Navy and its aircraft carrier battle groups in a precarious—but challenging—position. It is a time where flexibility, instinct, and ingenuity mean significantly more than reliance on technology and a rigid adherence to tradition. In spite of the differences in the operational environment, one thing remains the same: The aircraft carrier battle group is indeed the "Iron Fist" of naval warfare.

Chapter 2

Flight Deck

The Most Dangerous Place on Earth

The best way to describe the flight deck of an aircraft carrier is this: choreographed chaos. There's no better way to describe the pandemonium of rainbow-colored, goggled sailors running all over the deck like ants, the deafening noise of powerful jet engines blasting just feet away from you, the 50-knot gale threatening to rip the clothes off your body, the stench and slippery feel of JP-5 and hydraulic fuel on the supposed nonskid surface beneath your feet, and the whirring invisible blades spinning on helicopters and propeller-driven aircraft that anxiously await to behead you or slice you in half if you make the wrong move.

The flight deck is all of these things, and more. It is a brutally unforgiving environment that demands you be at 110 percent, or suffer the consequences. The flight deck is readily acknowledged as being the most hazardous workplace in the world. Simply put: People die if they make a mistake, and their deaths are anything but peaceful. Over the years, carelessness and poor concentration have been responsible for sailors being beheaded, mutilated, torched, sucked into jet engines, or blasted overboard.

Because of the ever-present danger, the flight deck is a Realm of Rules, and the monarch of that realm is the air boss. Perched some 60 feet above the

> ### *This is four-and-a-half acres of sovereign territory.*
>
> **Rear Admiral (Select) Lindell G. "Yank" Rutherford, Commanding Officer, USS** *George Washington* (CVN-73)

flight deck in a miniature aircraft control tower known as Primary Flight Control or "PriFly" for short, the air boss—wearing a fluorescent yellow shirt that has the words *Air Boss* boldly stenciled on the back—has an unobstructed view through the huge tinted-glass windows of the flight deck and everything to the port side of the aircraft carrier. Many sailors and pilots refer to the air boss as "God," because in a sense he is.

"I own all the airspace within 10 miles of this ship," says Commander Tim Alexander, air boss aboard the amphibious assault carrier USS *Nassau* (LHA-4). "Nothing happens unless I authorize it; no aircraft can launch or recover without my say so."

The air boss is assisted by a mini boss, who also sits in PriFly. Aboard an aircraft carrier, they orchestrate the launching and recovery of F-14 Tomcats, F/A-18 Hornets, SH-60 Seahawks, EA-6B Prowlers, S-3 Vikings, and E-2C Hawkeyes. On an amphibious assault carrier they deal with AV-8B Harrier "Jump Jets," CH-53E Super Stallions heavy lift helicopters, and AH-1W Super Cobra attack helicopters.

Moving large aircraft on the narrow, pitching flight deck of an aircraft carrier and jockeying them into position so they can be launched from one of the

A view from "vulture's row" on the island of two F/A-18 Hornets preparing to launch off the USS *Kennedy's* waist catapults. Launches are highly choreographed to ensure the safety of the dozens of flight crew needed to make a launch possible. Take note of the jet-blast deflector (JBD) behind the closest Hornet. It protects the crew and nearby jets from the jet's 2,300-degree exhaust, which has been known to scorch aircraft nosecones and melt cockpit canopies. The JBDs have an internal cooling system that uses seawater to prevent it from melting. Problem is, the seawater is corrosive, causing major maintenance headaches on all carriers. The problem will be addressed and, it is hoped, corrected on the CVN-77 and CVX carriers in the future. *S. F. Tomajczyk*

four steam catapults every 30 seconds is a demanding and delicate task. There is no room for error. This becomes even more apparent when an aircraft carrier is simultaneously launching *and* recovering aircraft. In these instances, during the day, two aircraft are being shot from catapults one and two on the bow,

Inside "PriFly" (Primary Flight Control) aboard the USS *George Washington*. This window—one of dozens—has been conveniently marked with a grease pencil to show key features of the flight deck so that new pilots ("nuggets") know what they're looking at when visiting the carrier for the first time. The aircraft in the background is a T-45 Goshawk, an advanced pilot trainer for both Navy and Marine Corps pilots. *S. F. Tomajczyk*

while an incoming aircraft is landing astern every 40 seconds. At night, they allow themselves 60 seconds to accomplish this feat.

"We have to have eyes all over our heads," explains Alexander. "We have to be aware of what's going on with the bow shots, how deck personnel are shuffling aircraft around on the deck or bringing up aircraft on elevators from below deck, and what the incoming aircraft is doing on its approach. [PriFly] is not a place where you can relax. It requires total concentration."

To help the air boss and mini boss, all personnel on the flight deck wear color-coded long-sleeve jerseys, helmets ("cranial"), and float coats. (A float coat is an inflatable vest. It is mandatory that all flight deck hands wear one in case they fall overboard. The 90-foot fall to the ocean's surface usually knocks people senseless, and they would drown without the float coat to keep their heads above water.) The different colors identify the specific task of the person.

For example, ordnance men ("Ordies" or "BB Stackers") wear red; aircraft refuelers ("Grapes") wear purple; arresting and catapult crews ("Frogs") wear green. The color-coding scheme enables PriFly to quickly determine at a glance of the flight deck if something is wrong or out of place, a visiting journalist (blue float coat) gawking in an area he doesn't belong in, for instance. If that happens, everyone will quickly know it. Using the PA system, the air boss will loudly ORDER the person to take corrective action . . . NOW! His booming voice drowns out the jet engines roaring on deck and can clearly be heard through the protective cranial, headphones, and earplugs everyone wears. Make the same mistake twice, and you're physically hauled off and banned from the flight deck. No one will be allowed to die because of your stupidity.

A Special Breed

If you think about it, you can't simply land a "normal" plane on an aircraft carrier flight deck. If you tried, it would crash and burn. First of all, the landing

An F/A-18 Hornet flies off the bow of the USS *John F. Kennedy,* its roaring engines set at military thrust. (Unlike the F-14 Tomcat, the Hornet does not need to go to full afterburner when launching.) Today's catapults can throw a Cadillac more than a half mile. This power is necessary to get a fully loaded fighter airborne in a mere 300 feet. The United States is one of the few nations in the world that has the technical and industrial skills to build catapults. *S. F. Tomajczyk*

runway is only 500 feet long—much too short for any aircraft to land on, save perhaps for a helicopter or an ultralight. Second, the ship is a moving target—steaming 20 to 30 knots ahead through the ocean while moving up, down, and sideways. It's extremely difficult to align the aircraft with the flight deck and make a clean landing.

Then there are all the other critical factors about naval aviation that drive aeronautical engineers crazy. Aircraft have to be rugged-ized to withstand the tremendous shock of launch and arrested landing ("controlled crash"). Hence, they are equipped with tailhooks, shockproof undercarriages, and low-speed

handling control surfaces. Additionally, the airframe itself must be light and strong, yet resistant to the corrosive effect of salt water.

To make things more challenging, the aircraft must fit on the flight deck elevators (which have size and weight limitations) and inside the hangar decks below. Since a carrier typically transports 75 aircraft, this means the planes have to fold somewhere to reduce their space requirements. This is why you see aircraft wings that can be folded, spindled, and muti-lated into yoga-like contortions. It also explains why helicopters have collapsible rotor blades and, some-times, tail sections.

PriFly is a busy and crowded area when flight operations are underway. This is illustrated by activities going on inside PriFly aboard the USS *George Washington*. PriFly is located atop the carrier's island where it has the best view of the flight deck and the surrounding ocean. The air boss, along with the mini boss, own all the airspace within 10 miles of the aircraft carrier. *S. F. Tomajczyk*

When launched from a catapult, an aircraft goes from 0 to 140 knots in less than three seconds. Most of the stress is on the front nose wheel. Conversely, when a plane lands using its tailhook, it goes from about 130 knots to 0 in two seconds (causing pilots' eyes to nearly pop out of their sockets). The primary stress in this case is in the tail section and fuselage frame. These extreme stresses are not the only two a naval aircraft experiences. The sink rate of a plane is about 28 feet per second as it approaches the stern of the aircraft carrier. As it slams onto the flight deck, the wings flex upward and then—almost

simultaneously—violently downward, causing them to travel through an arc of up to 3 feet.

With physics and Mother Nature actively influencing naval aviation, it is a wonder that the aircraft can even fly. This is especially true when you stand out on the flight deck and watch fully armed 72,000-pound F-14 Tomcats and 48,000-pound F/A-18 Hornets waiting in line to catapult off the bow. Carrier operations have a certain aura to them, and for good reason.

Launch!

When a carrier deploys overseas, it is accompanied by a carrier air wing (CVW) that is typically comprised of three F/A-18 Hornet fighter squadrons, one F-14 Tomcat fighter squadron, one S-3 Viking antisubmarine squadron, one EA-6B Prowler electronic warfare squadron, one E-2C Hawkeye airborne early-warning squadron, and one SH-60 Seahawk helicopter squadron. There are some 75 aircraft that fly aboard the carrier from various naval air stations a day or so after the carrier leaves port.

Each squadron brings its own aviators and support and maintenance crews. Sometimes this can be as many as 300 people, which is why a carrier swells from 2,000 to more than 5,500 personnel when it is deployed. The sailors assigned to the carrier are responsible for operating the ship and doing limited flight deck work, such as aircraft refueling, ordnance, crash and salvage, and aircraft handling. Everything else is done by the members of the squadrons. They are responsible for anything that deals directly with the aircraft, such as aircraft repair and maintenance, catapult hookups, and arrested wire recoveries.

When it comes time to launch aircraft, the procedure is influenced by the mission profile. For instance, if a carrier wants to extend its antisubmarine warfare (ASW) picket over the horizon, it will want to launch the Vikings or a LAMPS III Seahawk. By contrast, if a carrier is ordered by the Theater Commander to jam enemy missile radar in support of an Allied strike mission, it will launch the Prowlers.

CENTRALIA HIGH SCHOOL LIBRARY
CENTRALIA, WASHINGTON 98531

Flight deck control, located at the base of the island, coordinates all activities on the carrier's 4.5 acres of tarmac. The gents shown here "spot" the aircraft on a scale tabletop model of the USS *Kennedy*. Notice that many of the aircraft silhouettes on the spotting board have pins and bolts on them. The colored pins denote which launch group the aircraft will be included in, while the wingnut signifies that the aircraft either has a problem or its wing spread is being checked. Purple nuts represent various fueling operations. When it is placed sideways, it means the aircraft needs fuel; up, fueling is underway. *S. F. Tomajczyk*

War and high tension also influence the launch procedure. Oftentimes in these situations, a carrier routinely maintains some of its fighter aircraft on various alert response times so it can quickly launch against a threat: Alert 5, Alert 15, and Alert 30. That means the fighters must start launching from the flight deck within 5, 15, or 30 minutes of receiving a launch order. In these circumstances, the aircraft are positioned on the flight deck in the order in which they will be launched to save time.

Regardless of whether it is war or peacetime, however, it is Flight Deck Control (FDC) that actually orchestrates all the activity to get the aircraft ready for launching. From its busy station, which is located at the base of the carrier's island, the men and women spot aircraft on a scale model of the flight deck and order the various crews to do their tasks, such as refueling aircraft, loading or unloading ordnance (which is stored in magazines aboard the carrier), and guiding the planes across the deck to the catapults.

As the aircraft carrier turns into the wind and increases its speed to 30 knots in an effort to increase the relative wind speed down the flight deck, the FDC orders the crews to prepare the aircraft for launching.

Ordnance personnel (also called BB Stackers or Ordies) are easily identified on a flight deck by their red vests, jerseys, and cranials. They are the only people aboard the carrier who are allowed to touch weapons and load them aboard aircraft. Their vests—as with all vests worn by flight deck personnel—carry a whistle, a sea dye marker, a flashing-strobe beacon, and a CO_2 cartridge to inflate a built-in flotation tube. *S. F. Tomajczyk*

VEST	CRANIAL	
Color	*Color*	*General Role*
Blue	Blue	Aircraft handler/Tractor driver
Blue	White	Elevator operator
Blue	Yellow	Aircraft directors
Brown	Brown	Plane captain
Brown	Red	Helicopter plane captain
Green	Green	Arresting/catapult crew
Green	Yellow	Arresting/catapult officers
Green	White	Replenishment officer

VEST	CRANIAL	
Color	*Color*	*General Role*
Purple	Purple	Refueling
Red	Red	Ordnance/crash crew/EOD
White	White	Safety/medical/transfer crew
White	(None)	Landing signals officers
White	Green	Plane inspector
Yellow	Yellow	Plane director/handling officer
Yellow	Green	Catapult and arresting gear crew

Carriers generally launch aircraft in groups, identified as 1st Group, 2nd Group, and so on. A group can consist of anywhere from 10 to 20 aircraft, depending on the mission.

When an aircraft is ready to launch, it is guided by hand signals to one of the four catapults by a yellow-shirted plane handler. When the plane's nose-wheel is just behind the catapult shuttle, which resembles a crab-like fixture, a metal bar on the plane's nose-gear strut is lowered into the shuttle. This enables the catapult to literally pull the plane down the flight deck when it is fired.

While this is occurring, the hydraulic Jet-Blast Deflector (JBD) is raised directly behind the aircraft to prevent its jet engine blast from frying planes and torching personnel on the flight deck to the rear. The JBD contains an embedded cooling system through which seawater is pumped. This keeps the deflector itself from melting.

Green-shirted "frogs"—catapult crew members—scramble under the plane and attach another metal bar to its nose gear strut, this time to the rear. Called a "holdback," this mechanical arm allows a plane to rev its engines to full power, without it moving an

LAUNCH! When everything has been checked and double-checked, the catapult officer drops to one knee and points down the runway. This acrobatic move tells the "shooter" to press a button that signals the order to fire to the catapult controller a deck below. Here, an F/A-18 Hornet strapped into the USS *Kennedy's* catapult number one is about to go from 0 to about 140 knots in less than two seconds. *S. F. Tomajczyk*

A close-up look at an arresting wire found aboard the USS *George Washington*. There are four such wires strung across the stern area of the flight deck, each suspended about 4 inches above the tarmac by two metal plate "springs" to enable the aircraft's tailhook to easily snag it. (You can see the metal springs in this photo. They are located midway across the frame.) The cables are woven from high-tensile steel wire. Subjected to tremendous forces, they are only used for 100 landings before they are replaced. *S. F. Tomajczyk*

inch. Doing so, the plane will have tremendous thrust when the catapult is finally fired.

Now, just moments away from being shot off the bow of the carrier, another green shirt holds up a board with the plane's expected takeoff weight so that the pilot and catapult officer can both see it. Using hand signals, the pilot either confirms the weight—which is the total of the aircraft's base weight, plus fuel and ordnance—or revises it in 500-pound increments until it is correct. This is vitally important, because the steam pressure in the catapult is set to match the plane's takeoff weight and other factors, such as humidity, wind speed, and air pressure. If too much pressure is used, the catapult will literally rip the plane's nose gear off. Too little, and the plane will never reach takeoff speed and will be flung into the ocean directly in front of the advancing carrier. This is known as a "cold shot" or "cold cat," and no aviator wants to experience it.

In 1983, the crew of an A-6E Intruder attack aircraft aboard the USS *John F. Kennedy* (CV-67) suffered a cold shot. Fortunately, both the pilot and navigator were able to eject just before the Intruder plunged into the ocean. Of the two, the pilot was more fortunate: His parachute landed him on the flight deck right in front of the Jet Blast Deflector that he had been revving in front of just seconds before. The poor navigator, however, found himself snagged on the starboard side of the *Kennedy*, just aft of the island. For more than a half hour he hung there—being violently smashed against the hull—until rescue personnel finally found him.

Due to the potential, lethal nature of a cold shot, pilots and the catapult officers take aircraft weight very seriously. This is especially true with the F-14 Tomcat, the undisputed heavyweight of the flight deck. Empty, it weighs in at around 46,500 pounds. Add maximum fuel, and it jumps to 66,500 pounds. And then, when you finally add ordnance, it can become an obese 70,000-plus aircraft. The maximum weight an F-14 can be for a safe launch, and that's a relative word, is about 76,000 pounds. But you won't

The newer Nimitz-class carriers have two catapult launch control pods: one located on the waist and the other on the starboard bow. They are flush with the flight deck to reduce the risk to the crew should an errant aircraft run into them. In this photo, taken aboard the USS *George Washington,* you can also see the optical landing system ("lens") to the right. The "green shirt" is checking to make sure everything is secure before the approaching storm arrives. *S. F. Tomajczyk*

find too many pilots willing to do that. Why? The amount of thrust required to get that so-called "sumo wrestler" airborne in a mere 300 feet is not only unbelievable, but it is painful for the pilots to endure, because their eyes are plastered to the rear of their skulls and all their blood is shoved against their spinal cord.

"You start to see stars at 71,000 pounds," says one F-14 pilot. "After that, it starts getting nasty, real quick. I wouldn't want to do a 76."

Fortunately, most F-14s sacrifice the initial fuel load so they can take off at lighter weights, generally around the 67,000-pound range. They can always top off their fuel once they are airborne from either an S-3 Viking refueler (using buddy fuel pods) or an Air Force tanker like the KC-135.

When the pressure in the catapult reaches the appropriate level, there is a final safety check of the aircraft by the green shirts. If everything is okay, the catapult officer signals this to the pilot, who then increases the engines' thrust to either full military power or afterburner, snaps a salute to the catapult officer, and braces himself for the launch. The catapult officer drops to his knee and points down the deck, and the "shooter" presses a button that signals the order to fire to the catapult controller a deck below.

WHAM! The holdback is snapped and the aircraft is hurled down the catapult track. Two seconds later and some 300 feet down the flight deck, the tow bar pops out of the shuttle and the aircraft is on its own, with the pilot flying it off the carrier's bow.

Meanwhile, back on deck, the cycle repeats. A top notch crew can retract the shuttle and move the next plane into place on the catapult for launching in about two minutes. This means that if all four of a carrier's catapults are used, an aircraft can be

TRAP! A T-45 Goshawk catches the number two arresting wire aboard the USS *George Washington*. Before starting the recovery operation, the flight deck crew was ordered to remove the number four arresting wire so that "nugget" pilots would not learn a potentially dangerous habit. Pilots who trap on the number four cable place themselves at serious risk of colliding with the stern of the carrier ("ramp strike"). *S. F. Tomajczyk*

launched every 20 to 30 seconds. In other words, a group of 20 fighters can be in the air and on their way to intercept a hostile aircraft in less than 10 minutes.

Whenever a carrier launches its aircraft, the very first one that is launched—and the last one recovered—is the so-called "plane guard," a helicopter that serves in the role of search-and-rescue in case a fighter splashes. (No, it does not need a catapult to become airborne.) The plane guard is always followed by the E-2C Hawkeye and then by the aircraft that make up the 1st Group, 2nd Group, and so on. The Hawkeye is the carrier's eye in the sky, and it quickly gets into

position to track enemy targets and provide intercept information to the launching aircraft.

Controlled Crashes

While launching from a carrier is difficult, landing on one is a nauseous, heart-pounding experience. Time and again, research has shown that pilots are less stressed when flying in combat than when trying to land on the pitching, rolling deck of a carrier. Without question naval aviation's toughest maneuver, arrested recovery ("controlled crash") demands extreme precision and a cool head. It is a procedure

Pilots pray they never meet these folks: the carrier's fire and rescue squad. Driving a specially modified tractor ("pig") that is equipped with firefighting gear, these men are on constant stand-by status during flight deck operations. If a plane crashes or catches fire— and they have over the years—they rush in wearing special aluminized clothing to rescue the air crew. It's a dangerous task that can claim the lives of the unwary and careless. *S. F. Tomajczyk*

that is literally measured in microseconds and inches. Make a mistake, and you become flattop pizza.

Before the recovery of aircraft can begin, the flight deck needs to be respotted. In other words, as many aircraft as possible must be moved forward to clear the stern area and the 500-foot-long landing strip, which is angled 14 degrees to port. In the event that a carrier intends to launch *and* recover aircraft at the same time, which is often done in wartime, some planes and helicopters may have to be sent below into the hangars to make room on the flight deck. In these instances, the carrier's four elevators are put to good use.

Once the aircraft have been respotted, the carrier turns into the wind (if it hasn't already done so) and PriFly and the air traffic control center (ATCC) get busy. Planes approach the carrier in one of two ways: either straight in from about 20 miles out or after flying several so-called "racetrack" laps near the ship. As to which flight pattern is followed, it is determined by circumstances and by the ATCC, which controls all the airspace 10 to 50 miles away from the carrier. (If you'll recall, the air boss owns the airspace within 10 miles of the carrier.) The ATCC is located one level down from the flight

An F-14 Tomcat is catapulted off the bow of the USS *Dwight D. Eisenhower* (CVN-69). *U.S. Navy*

Notable Flight Deck Accidents

Pilot error is blamed for most aircraft accidents. A 1993 study by the Navy showed that of 6,700 Navy and Marine Corps aviation incidents between 1977 and the end of 1992, human factors contributed to most accidents. Mechanical failure virtually disappeared as a major cause. Interestingly, single-seat aircraft were found to be most likely to be involved in an accident when landing between 9 p.m. and midnight, and two-seat aircraft have half as many accidents as single-seat aircraft.

May 26, 1981: An EA-6B Prowler skids across the flight deck of the USS *Nimitz* and collides with other aircraft. Explosions and fires aboard the ship killed 14 and injured 42. The event occurred off the Florida coast.

September 6, 1981: An A-7E Corsair collides with a F-14 Tomcat while coming in for a landing on the USS *Kitty Hawk* in the Indian Ocean. One is killed and two are injured.

January 25, 1987: An EA-3B Skywarrior crashes into the deck of the USS *Nimitz* and skids into the Mediterranean Sea, killing seven.

October 29, 1989: A T-2 Buckeye flown by a pilot trainee on a training flight crashes on the deck of the USS *Lexington* in the Gulf of Mexico and starts a fire. Five are killed and 19 are injured.

July 20, 1993: An F-14 Tomcat crashes on the USS *Abraham Lincoln* in the Indian Ocean. One is killed and six are injured.

March 16, 1997: An F/A-18 Hornet crashes into the flight deck of the USS *John F. Kennedy* while operating off the North Carolina coast. Eight are injured. The collapse of the jet's landing gear caused the accident.

November 8, 1998: An EA-6B Prowler crashes while landing at night aboard the USS *Enterprise,* which was getting ready to deploy overseas. The 4 crewmen aboard the Prowler are killed and 12 flight deck personnel are injured. Additionally, 2 crewmen aboard an S-3 Viking barely escape death by ejecting just as the Prowler slams into their aircraft.

April 2, 1999: Two sailors are seriously injured aboard the USS *John C. Stennis* when a section of a 12,000-pound jet blast deflector falls on them while doing routine maintenance. One sailor has his leg amputated below the knee, while the other loses all of one leg.

The landing signals officer (LSO) assigned to fighter attack squadron 83 (VFA-83) guides an F-14B Tomcat in for a safe landing aboard the USS *Enterprise*. Throughout the approach, the LSO monitors the aircraft's position, ensuring that it is in the appropriate glide path. He can wave off the plane if its approach is erratic or if the flight crew has not cleared the runway fast enough. A carrier can recover an aircraft every 40 seconds. *U.S. Navy*

deck, usually near the ship's combat direction center for ease of data transfer.

If air traffic is heavy, the ATCC will stack the aircraft in an oval-shaped racetrack that measures about 1 mile wide and 4 miles long. This holding position is located to the port side of the carrier out near the horizon. Aircraft are placed into the stack based upon their fuel status: Those low on fuel get priority for landing. To prevent planes from actually running out

of fuel and splashing into the ocean, an airborne tanker—an S-3 Viking carrying a 300-gallon fuel tank and a hose-and-drogue pod—is positioned nearby to refuel anyone flying on fumes and a prayer.

To make carrier landings easier and less stressful on pilots, the Navy uses a variety of landing aids, including an optical landing system known as the "lens." The lens is located on the port side of the flight deck in a sponson. It is a stabilized system of

A Navy air traffic controller monitors the positions of pilots during flight operations from the aircraft carrier USS *Nimitz* (CVN-68). The *Nimitz* and its air wing (CVW-9) were operating in the Persian Gulf in support of Operation Southern Watch at the time. *U.S. Navy*

lights (meaning, they don't move with the ship) and directional lenses that enable pilots to avoid gliding in to the flight deck too high or too low. If an aircraft is at the proper attitude and sink rate, the pilot sees an amber light ("meatball"). By maintaining the "ball" centered all the way down (with a row of green lights, *not* red), then he will be in an ideal spot to land on the flight deck.

When it comes time for a pilot to land his aircraft, he breaks out of the racetrack pattern and heads for the stern, descending parallel to the carrier along the port side. During this downwind leg, the aircrew prepare for landing—lowering the flaps, landing gear, and tailhook. When the aircraft is a mile or so behind

the aircraft carrier, the pilot abruptly banks to the left in a 180-degree turn and drops down to 800 feet. This maneuver produces about 2 Gs of gravitational force on the aircrew. When the operation is completed, the plane will be 3/4 mile—about 20 seconds—from the carrier's flight deck.

At this point, the pilot will hear the landing signals officer (LSO) aboard the carrier order, "Call the ball." The LSO is a qualified pilot whose job is to monitor the plane's approach and to make sure the flight deck is clear for landing ("green deck"). He and his assistant(s) are located in a small platform near the port-side stern area of the ship. By ordering "Call the ball," the LSO is simply asking the pilot to confirm

As this photo shows, war is a 24-hour business. Flight crews often launch and recover aircraft at all hours of the night. This photo is of an F/A-18 Hornet launching from the deck of the USS *Enterprise* (CVN-65) during Operation Desert Fox in December 1998. You can better understand why flight deck crew members avoid the rear area of a jet aircraft. *U.S. Navy*

that he has the meatball in clear sight. If he does, he responds, "Roger ball."

The plane is now only 10 seconds from landing. From here on in, the LSO and his assistants carefully judge the aircraft's attitude and make certain that everything is safe. As part of this effort, the LSO is the only flight deck person who doesn't wear a cranial. Why? He needs all his senses to do his job, including the ability to hear the whining of the jet's engine as the plane approaches, as well as any last-minute warnings made by the air boss or flight deck personnel.

In his hand, the LSO holds a narrow, television remote–like device known as a pickle. It controls a

series of lights positioned near the LSO platform, which can be seen by incoming pilots. As long as the plane appears to be fine for a safe landing ("in the groove"), the pilot sees a glowing green light. If, however, corrective action needs to be taken, the LSO can use the pickle to activate the appropriate lights to convey the message (more power, for example). If things become really messed up, he can order the plane to stop its approach and give it another attempt. This is known as a "wave off," and it can be done not only by the LSO, but also by the air boss and mini boss who closely monitor landings from PriFly, some 60 feet above the flight deck.

By this time the jet finds itself nose up about 30 feet above the flight deck, approaching at a speed between 120 and 140 knots—far slower than its top speed, but fast enough to make things dicey, especially on windy days. As the aircraft roars in and finally slams onto the flight deck, the pilot aims to snag with his tailhook one of four, braided-steel arresting cables strung across the runway. They are positioned about 50 feet apart from each other.

Pilots are taught from day one to avoid the rearmost, first wire. To do so places the aircraft at great risk of striking the carrier's stern and crashing. This is known as a "ramp strike." (During naval aviator training, carriers often take down the first cable so that the pilots are not tempted to use it in the first place.) They are also taught to avoid the fourth—and last—wire because if they miss it there is less than 300 feet of tarmac remaining to regain takeoff speed. Hence, pilots aim for wire three. It gives the plane adequate room from the stern (meaning, no ramp strikes) and it provides maximum rolling distance to allow the plane to take off again if necessary.

As the plane's tailhook drags and skips along the flight deck searching for an arresting cable, the pilot opens up the throttle to full power. This enables him to take off again ("bolter") if for some reason the tailhook misses all the wires and he suddenly finds himself staring at the deep blue sea.

Once a cable is snagged ("trapped"), hydraulic ram buffers located one deck below and attached to either end of the cable, dampen the energy from the aircraft. The amount of tension placed on the cables is determined by the estimated landing weight of the plane. For instance, an F/A-18C Hornet in typical peacetime configuration weighs in at 42,000 pounds as it crosses the carrier's stern. By comparison, an F-14D Tomcat outfitted with a TARPS pod can easily weigh 71,000 pounds when it lands. Hence, more tension must be used to stop the heavier Tomcat in the same distance used to halt the lighter Hornet.

This hydraulic damper system brings the plane to an abrupt halt within 320 feet, in just two seconds. If the aircrew is not securely strapped in, they will find themselves spackled on the canopy or cockpit windows.

Once the jet is safely on the carrier and the pilot has throttled down the engine, a green-shirt "hook runner" runs out and clears the arresting wire from the tailhook so that it can be retracted in preparation for the next plane, which is only 30 to 40 seconds away. Meanwhile, a blue-shirt plane handler uses hand signals to direct the jet to an area of the flight deck where all ordnance is inspected by red-shirted BB stackers, and red-tagged safety pins are installed to prevent accidental detonation.

Immediately after each landing, and before the next aircraft is on its final approach, the LSO grades the pilot's landing, recording two scores. The first critiques the way in which the pilot flew the approach and landing. There are four grades: OK (excellent, safe flying); Fair (not good, but safe); No Grade (unsafe flying); and Cut (very unsafe flying that could have resulted in a crash).

The second score indicates which arresting cable the pilot snagged. As mentioned previously, the best cable for a pilot to trap is wire 3 since it is the safest. Trapping wires 2 or 4 is acceptable, but a score of lesser value is awarded. The lowest score is given to wire 1 traps since they are the most dangerous to both the aircrew and flight deck personnel.

Needless to say, all pilots strive to receive an "OK, Three" each time they land aboard a carrier. They know that their LSO scores affect their future promotion hopes. Those with high cumulative scores ("good hooks") are often sent to NAS Pensacola to become instructors, while others find themselves as test pilots at Patuxent River Naval Air Test Center in Maryland. Pilots who score low—especially with many wire 1 traps—may never find themselves in a cockpit again.

Naval aviation has enough risks and dangers. . . .

Command, Control and Intelligence
The Brains Behind the Brawn

> ### To be forewarned is
> ### to be forearmed.
>
> **Popular saying**

When discussing the awesome firepower represented by an aircraft carrier battle group, it is easy to forget that war is two-sided. America's naval forces respond to threats posed by potentially hostile forces and they, in turn, to our response. And so the tip-toe dance continues, with each opponent skillfully maneuvering and counter-maneuvering to avoid being vulnerable to attack.

It is important to remember that a successful military operation is not the result of a battle group being able to fire its guns, shoot its missiles, or launch its fighter aircraft. Granted, these capabilities are important, but they are reactive in nature. Instead, a successful operation is due to the CVBG's ability to proactively "see" the enemy first and to take advantage of his weaknesses without him knowing it—until it's too late. Because of this, a large portion of the battle group's resources are dedicated to constantly collecting and analyzing information about hostile military forces so the CVBG can respond effectively and decisively with lethal force should combat arise.

Every surface combatant within the battle group is a pincushion of antennas that passively receive what is known in military parlance as SIGINT—signals intelligence. SIGINT is divided into three types of activity: communications intelligence (COMINT), electronics intelligence (ELINT), and telemetry intelligence (TELINT). COMINT is concerned with intercepting, analyzing, and deciphering radio communications, while ELINT is involved with studying radar and noncommunications signals. TELINT covers the interception of telemetry data, which is generally associated with missiles (range, speed, course, and bearing).

The carrier battle group uses signals intelligence (which is constantly received 24 hours a day and analyzed by the Joint Intelligence Center and the Ships Signals Exploitation Space) to locate and identify the position of enemy ships, aircraft, submarines, command posts, shore-based weapons, and even spacecraft. By carefully monitoring the signals emitted by these targets, it is possible for the battle group to determine the types of radar, fire control systems, communication systems, and weaponry that a belligerent nation has fielded. It is even possible to anticipate what an enemy's strategy and tactics are by analyzing the location, movement, and density of the signals received.

For instance, the concentration of shore-based radio signals in a remote area of the Persian Gulf might warn of a new military command post or suggest that forces are gathering for a military operation.

Similarly, plotting the positions of surface-to-air missile (SAM) fire-control signals gives the battle

The combat direction center (CDC) is the heart and soul of the USS *George Washington*. Located directly under the reinforced flight deck for better protection against enemy attack, it is where all tactical information about the battle group is received for analysis and, ultimately, a response. As can be seen on the monitor at the upper left, live video camera coverage of aircraft landing on the flight deck can be monitored. In addition to this, displays in the large, air conditioned room show the carrier's location, speed, and heading, PLUS the status of its weapons systems and the positions of hostile and unknown targets. *S. F. Tomajczyk*

Behind this door is where the aircraft carrier battle group's or amphibious ready group's combat strategy is devised. Located near the CDC/CIC, the flag battle room is equipped with similar monitors that display vital tactical information. Live video-conferencing is also possible. The CVBG commander and his support staff meet here to discuss operational trends, intelligence information, and deployment/response strategies. *S. F. Tomajczyk*

group commander and the theater commander some insight into how the enemy deploys defensive weapons and where important military targets worthy of such anti-aircraft protection are located.

The carrier battle group supplements its SIGINT antennas with other means to quietly collect intelligence about its adversaries. The E-2C Hawkeye and EA-6B Prowler aircraft, for example, are routinely used to intercept signals intelligence over the horizon,

well beyond sight of the battle group. But when it comes time to get in close and dirty with the enemy, the CVBG relies on the F-14 Tomcat and—more recently—the F/A-18 Hornet to collect photographic intelligence while flying over hostile territory.

For these high-speed missions, the F-14 uses a detachable pod known as TARPS—Tactical Air Reconnaissance Pod System—to convert into a reconnaissance plane. The 1,700-pound pod is bolted into place beneath the fuselage in the starboard aft Phoenix missile station. It features a pair of forward- and down-looking framing cameras, a low-altitude panoramic camera, and an infrared line scanner for day/night visual reconnaissance duties. TARPS F-14s ("Peeping Toms") are used by the battle group to photograph terrain, conduct bomb-damage assessment (BDA), and monitor the enemy's location, size, strength, and activities. The pod does not interfere with the F-14's ability to defend itself: The aircraft is still able to carry a reasonable number of missiles for self-defense.

With advancements in technology, a digital version of TARPS has been developed. Called DI TARPS—the DI stands for "Digital Imagery"—the system enables the Tomcat to "fax" images over the airwaves via radio to the CVBG commander in near real-time. The digital camera system replaces the forward-looking camera found in the older TARPS pod.

According to Lieutenant (jg) Brian Hodges of VF-213 Blacklions, this means that the battle group commander can have aerial footage of a target within minutes, if not seconds. A scenario where DI TARPS would prove to be ideal is a situation where the enemy is constantly shuffling valuable assets around, such as a surface-to-air missile launcher. An F-14 combat air patrol launched from a carrier can photograph the SAM battery, send it back to the battle group via DI TARPS, and then receive authorization within minutes to destroy the target before the enemy is able to move it.

In May 1999, TARPS and DI TARPS received company from a digital imagery system called ATARS

(Advanced Tactical Airborne Reconnaissance System). The Marine Corps installed the experimental system in the nose cone of two F/A-18 Hornets deployed in the Balkans, replacing the 20-millimeter machine gun. ATARS was used on 38 missions during a three-week period. As the jets flew missions over an area, the system collected digital video footage, which was then analyzed by intelligence officers and used for planning. Like DI TARPS, ATARS can be used to provide pre- and poststrike target assessments, to search for surface-to-air early warning and fire-control radar, and to detect and classify targets—all in near real-time. The main difference between the two reconnaissance systems is that ATARS is not slung beneath the fuselage in a pod.

For high-risk missions, an aircraft carrier battle group can launch unmanned aerial vehicles (UAV) that are equipped with reconnaissance gear. The UAVs transmit data back to the CVBG while loitering over enemy territory. If it is shot down or mechanically fails, then there is no loss of human life. The Navy, and other military services, currently use the "Predator" UAV for surveillance purposes. Designed by General Atomics Aeronautical Systems (San Diego), the Predator provides day and night coverage with its optical, infrared, and synthetic aperture radar sensors. High-resolution color video of critical targets are passed via a Ku-band satellite link to theater commanders, Pentagon intelligence analysts, and controllers on the ground or aboard ships. The synthetic aperture radar provides Predator with an all-weather surveillance capability that is also relayed worldwide by satellite in real-time. Measuring 27 feet long with a wingspan of 48 feet, the Predator can fly at altitudes of 25,000 feet for up to 50 hours per mission, gathering intelligence.

Other American military UAVs that are of use and importance to naval operations include:

Global Hawk: A high-altitude, long-endurance craft designed to operate at altitudes up to 65,000 feet over low to moderate threat areas. With its 116-foot wingspan and 44-foot length, Global Hawk can carry

The E-2C Hawkeye ("Hummer") is the battle group's proverbial eye-in-the-sky. It is the first fixed-wing aircraft to fly off the deck of a carrier (and the last to recover), to provide fighter aircraft with intercept vectors to bogeys, if necessary. The Hawkeye is acknowledged as being the most difficult aircraft to land on a carrier due to the torque created by its props. (The plane's 80-foot, 7-inch wingspan doesn't help either. It's the largest among naval aircraft.) The easiest plane to land is the S-3 Viking since it has a low stall speed. *S. F. Tomajczyk*

a 2,000-pound payload, which includes both synthetic aperture radar (SAR) and electro-optical and infrared sensors. With the SAR, it is capable of surveying, in one day, an area equivalent to the size of the state of Illinois (40,000 square miles), while providing 3-foot resolution images to military field commanders in near real-time. If necessary, it can also take as many as 1,900 spot images of the ground at 1-foot resolution. Each photo covers a square area measuring 2 kilometers by 2 kilometers. The 24,000-pound Global Hawk, which the Pentagon likens to being a modern-day U-2 spy plane, has an endurance of 42 hours and a range of 14,000 miles. Currently, two Global Hawks are undergoing advanced technology demonstration testing with the U.S. Atlantic Command. The Navy has participated in that endeavor.

DarkStar: Resembling a B-2 Spirit bomber in appearance, DarkStar is intended to be Global Hawk's stealthy partner. A high-altitude, long-endurance UAV, DarkStar is designed for use in dangerous, highly defended areas where its low-observable technologies

43

The combat information center aboard the amphibious assault ship USS *Nassau* (LHA-4). *S. F. Tomajczyk*

help it thwart being detected by enemy forces. It has a gross weight of 8,600 pounds (about a third that of the Global Hawk) and can operate at just over a 45,000 altitude for more than eight hours. It has a range of 500 nautical miles. DarkStar, which is being developed by Lockheed Martin Skunk Works and Boeing Military Aircraft, took its maiden flight in March 1996. It is a fully autonomous system, capable of taking off and landing using the differential Global Positioning System. Although the DarkStar project was cancelled by the Air Force in 1999, the Pentagon is still in search of a high-altitude, long-endurance stealthy UAV to fill its shoes.

Outrider: This is a tactical UAV that is designed to provide lower military echelons with focused coverage of the battlefield, primarily through video. Fully deployable, Outrider will reportedly assist with target identification, provide laser designation, and create communication links without interfering with nearby friendly aircraft.

I Spy

At the national level, intelligence information is collected, analyzed, and disseminated by a variety of government and military agencies, including the CIA, National Security Agency, U.S. Air Force, and the National Reconnaissance Office. Much of this data is

obtained from satellites, which are capable of peering deep inside a nation's borders to learn what is going on. The better known satellites include:

The *Defense Support Program* (DSP, Code 647): A reconnaissance and early-warning satellite placed in geosynchronous orbit that uses infrared sensors to detect the launches of intercontinental/theater missiles and submarine-launched ballistic missiles, as well as nuclear detonations and routine satellite and test missile launches. There are three DSP satellites in orbit at any given time (plus two backups). They are stationed over the Indian Ocean, Brazil, and the central Pacific Ocean. Additionally, a fourth satellite is located some 400 miles off the coast of Ecuador. Its role is classified, but it may serve as a backup or be involved with military defense research.

The DSP satellites transmit their digitized data to one of two ground stations, one at Woomera AS in Australia (also called Nurrungar) and the other at Buckley Airfield in Colorado. From there, the data is relayed to NORAD and U.S. Space Command early-warning centers at the Cheyenne Mountain Complex in Colorado. (There is a simplified DSP processing station in Vogelweh, Germany, as well as six mobile ground stations based in New Mexico.) It is believed that the most recently launched DSP satellites are capable of transmitting missile warning and intelligence information to ground stations by a laser communications system.

During Operation Desert Storm in 1991, the DSP satellite stationed over the Indian Ocean detected the launch of Iraqi SCUD missiles and provided early warning to civilian populations and coalition forces in Saudi Arabia and Israel. Analysts were able to determine the missile's launch point, the type of missile that it was, and where the likely impact point would be based on its trajectory. The nearest Patriot missile battery in Saudi Arabia was then alerted so that it could intercept and destroy the SCUD in flight.

The military has wanted to replace the aging DSP satellites since the early 1990s, but Congress has refused to fund any of the various proposed sys-

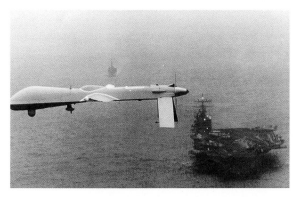

The Navy is becoming more reliant on unmanned aerial vehicles (UAV) to collect tactical information about enemy forces. The Predator is one of several UAVs in use with the U.S. military. It is shown here flying above the USS *Carl Vinson* (CVN-70) on a simulated reconnaissance mission off the coast of San Nicholas Island in southern California. The Predator provides near real-time infrared and color video to intelligence analysts on the carrier. *General Atomics Aeronautical Systems Inc.*

tems. It now appears, however, that a new, space-based infrared system (SBIS) will reach initial operational capability in 2002. Very little is known about this classified satellite system except that it appears to have three elements: two highly elliptical orbiting satellites, four geosynchronous satellites, and an unknown number of low-Earth-orbiting satellites.

Keyhole (KH): This is a codename for a series of area-surveillance, photographic reconnaissance satellites operated by the Air Force and CIA since the 1960s. The primary mission of these low-orbiting satellites is to acquire imagery intelligence (IMINT).

There are two Keyhole satellite variants in operation today: KH-12 Ikon and Lacrosse. The KH-12 uses digital imaging with a resolution of about 3 inches. This allows the Ikon to perform both high-resolution and area surveillance; photos are relayed to ground stations in real-time.

The Lacrosse satellites are similar to the KH-12, but have a synthetic aperture radar on board. This allows them to "see" through clouds and darkness and produce radar-like images.

Both the KH-12 Ikon and Lacrosse satellites can be launched into orbit by a Titan III booster or the Space Shuttle. Once in orbit, they can be serviced by shuttle astronauts to extend their lifetime.

Magnum: A signals intelligence satellite designed to intercept military communications and to collect missile telemetry. The $300 million, 5,000-pound geosynchronous satellite reportedly has two large dish antennas: One compiles telemetry, radar, and radio transmissions, while the other relays data to a ground station at Alice Springs in Australia.

Teal Ruby: An infrared sensing system housed aboard a satellite known to the Air Force as "Project 888." The sensor can detect aircraft in flight over the Earth's surface. It works by scanning the lower atmosphere in a grid-like fashion searching for the thermal signatures of airborne planes.

Vortex: A geosynchronous orbit SIGINT and TELINT satellite system used to eavesdrop on communications worldwide. Vortex satellites are reputed to be sensitive enough to intercept signals from low-power transmitters, such as walkie-talkies.

White Cloud: In addition to the aforementioned satellite programs, the U.S. Navy has its own satellite surveillance system. Codenamed Classic Wizard, it passively monitors foreign naval activities at sea by detecting the surface ships' signals emissions and then using triangulation to determine their position. This system enables aircraft pilots and antiship missiles to find their targets once they are directed to the correct area.

Classic Wizard consists of a space-based component—"White Cloud" satellites—and a worldwide ground network of receiving and transmitting stations, which are operated by Naval Security Groups. Each White Cloud satellite is made up of a mother satellite and three small subsatellites. Once the mother satellite is in orbit 700 miles above the Earth's surface, the three subsatellites are released. They then spread out to cover a wider area. Each cluster is capable of detecting ship transmission from as far away as

The USS *Nimitz* (CVN-68) launches chaff in a last-ditch effort to fool an incoming antiship missile. Chaff can be deployed around a ship out to a distance of 6,500 feet so that the missile will lock on to the false-return signal. Chaff was developed during World War II to protect bomber forces; it was made from strips of aluminum foil. The chaff bloom shown here was done as part of an exercise conducted off the southern coast of California in 1995. *U.S. Navy*

As illustrated by Operation Desert Storm in 1991, domination of the battlespace is the ultimate goal in warfare. If your forces control the sea, land, and air, you are able to dictate when, where, and how you will fight the enemy—to his disadvantage. In modern warfare, military units are completely dependent on electronic systems to operate equipment, to detect and locate threats, to launch and control weapons, and to communicate with units and higher military authority. If any of these is disrupted for a long enough time, or at a critical moment, it could mean the demise of the military unit.

The primary means of achieving control over the battlespace is to take control of the electromagnetic spectrum (sonar and ELF radio at the lower end of the spectrum to lasers in the high end). In essence, this means that a military force, such as a carrier battle group, takes actions to (1) hinder and disrupt the enemy's use of the spectrum, (2) obtain intelligence from the enemy's use of the spectrum, and (3)

A War of Electrons and Chaff

protect one's use of the spectrum from being disrupted by the enemy. Collectively, this is known as electronic warfare, and it is a battle that is fought with electrons.

For a CVBG, this means that it uses SIGINT antennas to locate enemy transmitters and then jam or deceive them with powerful signals. The most powerful electronic warfare asset aboard a carrier is the EA-6B Prowler. Carrying up to five jamming pods, it is routinely used to provide an umbrella of protection for strike aircraft and warships against enemy missile radar. The Prowler jams the radar so that the enemy is unable to lock a firing solution on the planes or ships.

In the event the enemy is able to launch a missile, chaff is often used to confuse it. Chaff is extremely thin (0.1 millimeter in diameter) aluminized glass fibers or silvered nylon fibers that are dispensed in bundles from aircraft or expelled from warships by shell or rocket. When the bundles burst open in the airstream, it forms a compact reflective cloud of suspended fibers that create false radar targets and break the lock of tracking radar systems. The length of the chaff used varies; the optimal length is about half the wavelength of the radar signal expected to be encountered. Due to the size and weight of the chaff, the filaments descend at a rate of only 1 or 2 feet per second. As a result, chaff clouds are long lasting, increasing the odds that the incoming missile will focus on it rather than the aircraft or warship.

Another system used aboard ships to fool radar-guided cruise missiles is the SLQ-17. It is a deception jammer affixed to the mast of a carrier, cruiser, or destroyer that generates an offset radar image of the ship. This means that an incoming cruise missile "sees" the fake radar return and homes-in on it rather than the real ship several hundred feet away.

One of the newest electronic countermeasures is the NULKA Mk-53 decoy launching system. Resembling a large pencil in shape with a small cross glued to one end, the NULKA is launched from a warship's deck when an incoming radar-guided missile is detected. Using a rocket, the decoy cartridge arches up into the sky where an internal emitter confuses the missile's tracking and homing system so that it misses the ship.

To prevent enemy forces from detecting a carrier battle group's electronic emissions and then capitalizing on it, all surface ships of the CVBG have the ability to control exactly how much electromagnetic radiation is emitted at any given time. In the ship's combat information center, personnel have the ability to reduce the emissions with the twist of a dial. Technicians constantly monitor how "noisy" the ship is, and they possess the authority to shut down systems within the ship to make it electronically quieter to thwart detection by enemy forces.

An inside look at a portion of the combat information center aboard the guided-missile cruiser USS *Cape St. George* (CG-71). The powerful AEGIS combat system, which essentially provides a 250-mile protective bubble over the carrier battle group, displays friendly, hostile, and unknown targets on the display screens. Multimission cruisers like the *Cape St. George* often play the Redcrown role in the battle group, constantly monitoring the airspace for enemy attack. *S. F. Tomajczyk*

2,000 miles. (White Cloud is also equipped with an infrared scanner to detect warm water discharged from a submerged nuclear submarine's reactor.)

The Navy has several White Cloud clusters in orbit at any given time, providing commanders with up to a dozen target-position reports each day. The satellites transmit this data regularly to ground stations, where it is analyzed and then sent on to naval commands and ships at sea, including carrier battle groups.

Spreading the Word

Once intelligence information is collected and analyzed, it does no one any good if it is locked away. Knowing what opponent military forces are doing can save lives by either preventing conflicts from arising in the first place or dramatically shortening the length of combat. Hence, the data must be shared with the appropriate naval leaders throughout the fleet. This can be accomplished through a number of ways, including the use of secure communication satellites. Two of the better known systems are DSCS and FLTSATCOM.

The Defense Satellite Communications System (DSCS) is a network of superhigh frequency, secure satellites that enable high-priority messages and data transmission to be sent. These include the exchange of wartime information between the National Command Authorities (NCA) and battlefield commanders, naval warships, and submarines, ICBM launch control centers, airborne command posts, overseas bases, and U.S. embassies. There are six 2,500-pound DSCS III satellites in geosynchronous orbit over the Atlantic, east and west Pacific, and Indian oceans. They send their data to 635 fixed, transportable, and mobile terminals on Earth, as well as to five DSCS operations control centers. DSCS, which can be launched into orbit from the Space Shuttle using a quasi-booster rocket known as an Inertial Upper Stage, is expected to remain in operation until at least 2005.

Aircraft carrier battle groups also use the Fleet Satellite Communications System (FLTSATCOM), a UHF and SHF system that allows all Navy ships, submarines, aircraft, and shore stations to communicate with each other. The five 4,136-pound FLTSATCOM satellites, which are in geosynchronous orbit over the equator, are currently being replaced by MILSTAR (Military-Strategic/Tactical Relay). It is an advanced, highly survivable EHF satellite system developed by the Air Force to ensure that the president and U.S. military commanders are able to communicate anytime, anywhere in the world—as well as to command America's strategic and tactical forces. Currently, the MILSTAR constellation has six satellites: two MILSTAR I satellites (which were launched in 1994 and 1995) and four more advanced MILSTAR II satellites. The MILSTAR II variant has a higher-capacity, medium-data rate than MILSTAR I to speed the flow of communications.

In spite of these excellent communications systems, the Navy recognizes that more needs to be done in the way of integrating systems and sharing data in

Blue lighting helps increase the contrast of cathode-ray tube displays in the CIC aboard the destroyer USS *Stump* (DD-978), making it easier for radar operators (shown here) to identify incoming aircraft and antiship missiles. *S. F. Tomajczyk*

both a lateral and vertical manner, not only among its own commands but, more important, with other armed forces. This is especially true in today's joint-force–minded military, where the Navy, Army, Air Force, and Marines are expected to meld into a single fighting force when deployed.

One of the first steps the Navy took was an experiment called "Challenge Athena I" that was first tested on the USS *George Washington* (CVN-73). It was a two-way, low-speed satellite link based on commercial antenna technology, and it was mainly used for video conferencing and sending and receiving intelligence data and images. The experiment was successful, and upgrades to the system were made quickly. Today, Challenge Athena III is being installed on carriers,

major surface combatants, fleet flagships, and amphibious assault ships. It offers the same features as the original system, but it also allows for two-way e-mail and direct, live access to commercial television channels. A similar version is being developed for underwater use by the Navy's submarine force to support special operations, Tomahawk-cruise-missile targeting, and other missions.

While Challenge Athena III enables the fleet to communicate among itself and the world, a new program known as IT-21 (Information Technology for the 21st Century) is well underway. Its long-term goal is to enable voice, video, and data transmission from a single desktop computer and allow the user to exchange classified and unclassified tactical

The EA-6B Prowler, shown here being refueled aboard the USS *Kennedy,* is the battle group's most powerful electronic-warfare air-craft. It is used to detect and jam enemy weapons' radar systems (such as surface-to-air missile launchers), as well as communication systems. The Prowler, staffed by a crew of four, often escorts combat air patrols and strike forces over hostile territory to prevent them from being shot down. During Operation Allied Force in 1999, the Prowler was even used to protect Air Force F-117 and B-2 stealth aircraft flying combat missions over Kosovo after an F-117 Nighthawk was shot down. *S. F. Tomajczyk*

information from the same workstation. IT-21 envisions a system that uses commercial off-the-shelf technology, as well as an Internet-like browser to permit the user to search and find specific information in databases that will be moved ashore.

Needless to say, IT-21 is an ambitious program, but it has received the enthusiastic support of the Navy's senior brass and is progressing well. In the Pacific, IT-21 has been implemented within the Kitty Hawk battle group and its attached amphibious ready group. It's also aboard two Joint Task

Force command ships, the USS *Blue Ridge* and the USS *Coronado.*

In the Atlantic, the USS *Enterprise* and her battle group ships were outfitted with the IT-21 satellite data transmission package in 1998. A subsequent deployment overseas proved that the destroyers and cruisers accompanying the *Enterprise* were attuned for the first time to all developments within the battle group. Data, instructions, and information were speedily passed from the CVBG commander to ship captains via secure e-mail instead of bringing them all together for a meeting on the flagship. The ease and speed of communication improved military operations and enabled commanders to remain in close contact with each other.

The Navy is now working to expand the high-speed IT-21 system across the fleet.

Combat Information Center

With the constant flow of data swamping the battle group, how do the warships sift through it all and figure out what is important, while at the same time being alert to respond to enemy attack? The answer is hidden in the bowels of the ship, behind locked hatches.

Welcome to the combat information center (CIC) or, depending on what type of warship you visit, the combat display center or combat direction center. Regardless of what you call it, they all have the same mission: to be ever vigilant for hostile targets and to quickly and effectively coordinate the ship's offensive and defensive efforts.

When you visit a CIC the first thing you notice (besides everyone scurrying around to cover up classified information) is that it is a dark and frigid room, eerily lit with pale-blue lights. Additionally, it is a cramped room filled with consoles and workstations that glow with fluorescent ruby, tangerine, and lime-green buttons and monitors. The entire visual effect—accompanied by a constant electronic hum of the powerful computers—makes you feel as if you are in a *Star Wars* epic movie.

Aboard most surface ships, such as cruisers and destroyers, the CIC is located several levels below and aft of the bridge, while aboard amphibious assault ships such as the *Tarawa* (LHA 1-5) and *Wasp* (LHD 1-6) classes, the CIC is safely positioned beneath the massive island structure. As for aircraft carriers, the CIC is below the heavily reinforced flight deck. You can hear the arresting cables and jet engines screaming through the ceiling every time an aircraft is trapped.

The thing to note here is that the CIC is intentionally located in a safe place (if any place aboard a warship can be considered safe) to ensure its survival

A carrier's island—like this one aboard the USS *Kennedy*—bristles with antenna for SIGINT, air traffic control, communications, and so on. It is also home of the ship's helm and navigation centers, as well as observation suites for the carrier air group commander (CAG), the carrier's commanding officer, and, from time to time, the admiral responsible for the battle group. It should be noted that the *Kennedy* is a test bed for the Advanced Combat Direction System (ACDS), a high-tech system that is supposed to give aircraft carriers and selected amphibious warfare ships state-of-the-art war fighting capabilities. ACDS, in development since 1994, is a computer system that, when linked with other naval tactical data systems, provides a battle group-wide picture of the threat environment. *S. F. Tomajczyk*

and operation in the event of enemy aircraft strafings, missile explosions, and underwater mine detonations. That is because the CIC is the nerve center of the ship: All information flows into it for analysis and, ultimately, a response.

The ES-3A Shadow replaced the EA-3B Skywarrior electronic reconnaissance aircraft in 1991. Sixteen of these modified Viking aircraft were delivered in pairs to aircraft carriers so they could conduct electronic surveillance, over-the-horizon targeting and C3I. They were principally used to extend a CVBG's threat detection and identification zone. The last of the Shadows were retired in August 1999. Their mission will be picked up by land-based EP-3 ELINT aircraft and spy satellites. *U.S. Navy*

The typical CIC is made up of various modules, which are located around the periphery of the CIC's main display area. Each of these workstations represents an aspect of warfare that is vital to the survival of the ship, including antisubmarine warfare, surface warfare, air combat, electronic warfare, and the ship's weapons fire control.

These mini–command centers monitor the raw or processed data that is forwarded to them by the ship's sensors. For example, in the ASW module, data from the ship's bow-mounted sonar system, variable depth sensors, and the towed sonar array (also called "the noodle") are processed and analyzed, including the identification of any sonar contacts by submarine class.

Final determinations from all modules are then forwarded to the display and decision area of the CIC, whose consoles face a wall lined with huge color monitors. Here, the CIC watch officer and tactical operations officer (TAO) can monitor, in near real-time, the ocean and air environment surrounding the warship or, in the case of an aircraft carrier, the battle group.

On one display, an overhead view of the ship's location is shown, with all targets—ships and aircraft—clearly identified. With a simple click of a computer mouse, the TAO can zoom in on a particular target and see data about its range, heading, and speed in relation to the warship. If the target is an aircraft, its IFF code appears on the screen to identify it as a friendly aircraft, not a hostile one.

Without a doubt, the most important component of the CIC is the AEGIS combat system, which is found aboard Arleigh Burke–class destroyers and Ticonderoga-class cruisers. Named after the mythological shield of Zeus (Greek god of the heavens and the earth), AEGIS is an anti-air warfare system that unites computers, radar, and missiles to provide a 260-mile defensive umbrella over the ship or battle group. It can automatically detect, track, and destroy numerous airborne, seaborne, and land-launched weapons simultaneously. The system's tracking capacity is in excess of 100 targets.

At the heart of this system is the powerful (4 megawatt), multifunction, phased-array SPY-1 radar. It is capable of combining the azimuth and height search, target acquisition, classification, and tracking functions.

In carrier battle groups, AEGIS data received and processed by the Arleigh Burke- and Ticonderoga-class ships are forwarded to the aircraft carrier's CIC so that the battle group commander can monitor and control the CVBG's response to threats.

In the past decade, the Navy has invested more than $350 million in a series of improvements to enhance AEGIS' theater missile defense capabilities as well as its ability to detect incoming antiship cruise missiles that are flying a few feet above the ocean's surface.

One of the more intriguing efforts now being undertaken by the Navy to improve the lethality of its battle groups is to merge AEGIS into a wireless network of sensor systems known as CEC, or cooperative engagement capability. CEC is intended to allow warships to pass tactical information from one ship to

The USS *Blue Ridge* (LCC-19) and USS *Mount Whitney* (LCC-20) are specialized command facilities for the amphibious fleets in the Pacific and Atlantic oceans. They are lined with a variety of surveillance, ECM/ESM, and communications aerials. The USS *Blue Ridge* is the flagship of the Seventh Fleet; USS *Mount Whitney* is the flagship of the Second Fleet. They are fitted with a tactical flag command center. *U.S. Navy*

another in real-time, much like the way a football quarterback laterals or throws the football to a receiver.

As with all tactical data, CEC/AEGIS information will be processed and put on display in a ship's combat information center.

When AEGIS is finally integrated into this network it will enhance the fighting and survival capability of individual ships. For instance, suppose a destroyer detects an antiship missile flying from shore toward another destroyer positioned 20 miles away on the horizon. Today, all the destroyer crew can do is alert the other warship and pray that it is able to quickly detect the missile with its own sensors and shoot it down. With CEC/AEGIS, however, the destroyer can continue to track the missile and relay the data to the threatened destroyer, which then fires on the missile using the relayed information.

CEC will also allow a battle group to divvy up tracking duties. For example, one CEC-equipped destroyer might focus its radar to detect low-flying cruise missiles, while another protects the CVBG from high-altitude attacks.

At this writing, a less capable version of CEC has been tested aboard the aircraft carrier *Eisenhower*, the amphibious assault ship *Wasp*, and the cruisers *Anzio*, *Hue City*, *Vicksburg*, and *Cape St. George*. Optimism over the tactical possibilities presented by CEC is high. As Lieutenant Ed Devinney, combat systems officer aboard the USS *Vicksburg*, was quoted in *Navy Times*, the new battle network system "is the best thing to hit the surface fleet in 50 or 60 years."

Chapter 4

Air Warfare
Dogfights and Fur balls

"It's difficult to sort out aircraft in close combat," a tactical action officer aboard the guided missile cruiser USS *Cape St. George* (CG-71) says as he peers at the computer-display screen in the ship's combat information center. It is filled with color-coded symbols that represent friendly, hostile, and unknown aircraft zipping around the protective "bubble" enveloping the battle group. "On the screen, they knot into a fur ball of friendlies and hostiles and come out as unknowns. I look at the blips and ask myself, 'Who are the good guys? Who are the bad?' I can't start shooting until I make sure they're not ours."

Such is the dilemma facing the *Cape St. George* as it plays the Redcrown role for an aircraft carrier battle group. Positioned near the aircraft carrier at the heart of the CVBG, the *Cape St. George* is responsible for anti-air warfare—constantly searching the skies for enemy aircraft and missiles. It is a defensive posture, but it is an important one since trouble can appear at any time. Incoming enemy fighters, for instance, can close at 20 miles per minute. So it is vitally important to the safety of the CVBG that the *Cape St. George* be able to clearly—and quickly—separate the friendlies from the hostiles, and then

I don't know about you, but I don't want a Navy full of fighter pilots who've been to a sensitivity seminar. I want mad-dog, rabid killers going to battle for me and mine. Men and women.

Drew Carey, comedian

direct the battle group's weapons fire against enemy aircraft.

In naval air warfare, Redcrown represents the last effort of a battle group to protect itself from aerial attack by a hostile force. The first line of defense is the responsibility of the carrier's fighters, F-14 Tomcats and F/A-18 Hornets. Flying combat air patrol (CAP), two or more fighters are positioned 100 miles or so down the line of the enemy's most likely direction of attack. These aircraft are controlled by the aircraft carrier itself, by an E-2C Hawkeye airborne early-warning plane, or by an outlying escort warship.

The role of CAP is to identify unknown approaching aircraft and to engage and shoot down hostile aircraft before they can launch their missiles at the battle group. As might be expected, going face-to-face with the enemy in a dogfight is a dangerous proposition, marked with speed, intuition, sharp yanks and banks, and an overdose of adrenaline. Only the skilled and persistent survive.

This chapter gives an overview of modern naval air warfare, both offensive and defensive. An aircraft carrier's air wing (CVW), which is made up of about 70 aircraft, has long been held in esteem by military

An F-14 Tomcat air superiority fighter from the Blacklions (VF-213) taxis out on the runway of NAS Oceana, Virginia, as it participates in a training exercise. When a carrier air wing is not deployed, its squadrons are land-based at various air stations around America where they undergo personnel changes and training. There are 10 air wings to service 12 combat carriers (not all of which are at sea), on a rotating basis. The typical air wing spends six months at sea conducting flight operations from the carrier, followed by 24 months ashore. *S. F. Tomajczyk*

The F/A-18E Super Hornet is the Navy's newest strike fighter. It is shown here conducting its first in-flight tests while loaded with two 2,000-pound bombs, two AGM-88 High Speed Anti-Radiation (HARM) missiles, and two AIM-9 Sidewinder air-to-air missiles. The Super Hornet will replace the A-6 Intruder and, eventually, the F-14 Tomcat. Compared with the earlier C/D models of the Hornet, the Super Hornet can fly 40 percent farther on a typical interdiction mission and can remain on station 80 percent longer during a typical combat air patrol. It also has increased engine power and more weapons stations. *U.S. Navy*

leaders, and for good reason. It is the tip of the spear where naval combat is concerned.

The Air Wing

When you stroll the flight deck of an aircraft carrier, you notice that there are six types of aircraft aboard parked in clusters at specific locations around the deck. Collectively, these aircraft represent the air wing assigned to the carrier during its six-month deployment overseas. The mix of aircraft gives the carrier flexibility and power in responding to different combat situa-

tions. A typical air wing consists of three F/A-18 Hornet squadrons, one F-14 Tomcat squadron, one S-3B Viking squadron, one EA-6B Prowler squadron, one E-2C Hawkeye squadron, and one SH-60 squadron. The size of the squadron varies by aircraft type.

The following chart gives the composition of a representative carrier air wing:

Aircraft	Mission
14 F-14 Tomcat	Air superiority, precision strike, reconnaissance
36 F/A-18 Hornet	Air superiority, precision strike, ground attack
4 E-2C Hawkeye	Airborne early warning, surveillance
4 EA-6B Prowler	Electronic warfare
6/8 S-3B Viking	Antisubmarine warfare, in-flight refueling
4/6 SH-60 Seahawk	Antisubmarine warfare, search and rescue

68 to 72 Total Aircraft

(Note: The air wing once had two ES-3A Shadow electronic reconnaissance aircraft assigned to it. These modified S-3A Viking aircraft were retired and placed in mothballs at Davis-Monthan Air Force Base in August 1999.)

The Navy maintains 10 air wings, each with six types of aircraft, for its 12 combat carriers. Each air wing is commanded by a Navy captain who is known to everyone as "CAG": commander, air group. Contrary to popular belief, he is a partner and an equal to the aircraft carrier's commanding officer, *not* a subordinate. They both report to the admiral (usually a two-star rear admiral) who commands the CVBG. The Navy deliberately organized its hierarchy this way so that flight operations are always controlled by trained aviators, not a senior officer who has never sat in a cockpit. So in a battle group, the CAG is responsible for

An F-14 Tomcat releases a GBU-24B/B hard target penetrator, laser-guided bomb while in a 45-degree dive during ordnance separation testing at NAS Patuxent River, Maryland. The bomb is designed to deeply penetrate the earth before detonating. It is an ideal weapon to use when attacking buried command posts and bunkers. *U.S. Navy*

the air wing and flight operations, while the aircraft carrier CO is responsible for his ship and the support services it provides to the air wing.

The majority of aircraft in an air wing are fighters—a total of 50 Tomcats and Hornets. This is not a mistake. The multirole fighter is the heart and soul of an air wing. It is able to engage enemy aircraft as well as attack ground targets with precision-guided munitions (PGM). This reflects the trend in naval aviation to have fewer, less-specialized aircraft. Over the next two decades, this course will result in the replacement of the EA-6B Prowler, F-14 Tomcat, and S-3B Viking with variants of the Joint Strike Fighter, which is now under development. (See the "Joint Strike Fighter" sidebar on page 65.)

When an aircraft carrier deploys overseas for its six-month cruise, the various squadrons that make up the air wing fly out to the carrier from their bases.

This usually happens a day or so after the carrier leaves the pier. The pilots carefully land their aircraft on the flight deck, where squadron and flight deck personnel reposition them for launching or storage in the hangar deck. While the pilots and air crew get the luxury of an extra day's vacation at home, the rest of the squadron (mechanics and LSOs) have to board the carrier when it's pier-side and get everything in order for flight operations. They move aboard all the squadron's equipment, including diagnostic gear and spare parts for the aircraft. The only things they do not bring are ordnance (bombs and missiles) and aviation fuel; those are provided by the carrier and the battle group's replenishment ship.

After the air wing is aboard the aircraft carrier, the CAG then initiates carrier qualifications ("carquals") for several days off the coast of the United States to ensure that the pilots, air crews, and flight deck crew are comfortable with launch and recovery operations since it may have been several weeks since their last exercise. Once carquals are over, the carrier is deemed ready to conduct air combat and the CVBG heads overseas. For the next six months, every day and night is filled with combat air patrols, battle exercises, and emergency drills. The goal of the battle group commander is to have a finely honed military fighting force at his disposal to enforce America's foreign-policy commitments and, if necessary, to wage war against hostile nations.

Fight Me If You Can

Americans have a love affair with the jet fighter. Why? It's fast. It's sleek. It's lethal. The jet fighter is the Lamborghini of the skies (albeit a heavily armed version). Attend any air show and you will see people's eyes light up in adoration and excitement whenever a fighter scorches the air above them, rattling their bones in the process. People will clap and shout and scream with delight. Jet fighters make people feel patriotic.

For more than two decades, the Northrop Grumman F-14 Tomcat has been the Navy's supreme

Pilots begin arriving at the "Ready Room" aboard the USS *George Washington* at 0500 hours to receive their preflight briefing and to finish putting on their equipment. At the back of the room and to the left is another small room where the Tactical Aircrew Mission Planning System (TAMPS) is located. TAMPS is a computer system that allows air crews to perform route and mission planning. The system takes into consideration things like enemy SAM launcher positions and missile ranges, as well as terrain features that can hide ("mask") the aircraft. When the TAMPS mission plan is finalized, it is reviewed, modified, and approved by the air-wing staff. *S. F. Tomajczyk*

air-to-air combat fighter, capable of shooting the lips off enemy planes at distances more than 100 miles away. The largest and heaviest fighter aircraft on the carrier flight deck—up to 74,000 pounds gross weight, depending on configuration, nearly 22,000 pounds more than an F/A-18D Hornet—the Tomcat is a two-seated, twin-engine fighter that is used for fleet air defense, interdiction, and strike missions. It features an auto sweep wing, which constantly readjusts the wing shape to give the flight crew the optimum performance for any maneuver they are performing. The wings sweep forward to increase aerodynamic lift in low-speed flight (catapult launch and carrier recovery), and they sweep back for reduced drag at high speeds, allowing the Tomcat to scorch through the skies at Mach 2.4. The normal sweep range is 20 to 68 degrees, with a

75-degree oversweep position that allows the aircraft to be stored in the carrier's hangar.

The F-14 is equipped with a long-range, pulse-Doppler radar (AWG-9 weapons control system) that can detect enemy fighters out to 195 miles. It is able to simultaneously track up to 24 targets and engage 6 of them flying at heights up to 80,000 feet and traveling at speeds of up to Mach 2.8 with AIM-54 Phoenix missiles at more than 60 miles away. A forward-looking, 30-degree field-of-view television camera site is fitted under the chin of the Tomcat, allowing the radar intercept officer (RIO), who sits in the rear tandem seat of the fighter, to visually identify targets 9 miles away before initiating an attack.

Visually, the Tomcat is an imposing aircraft to look at when it's fully armed. It has a six-barrel, 20-millimeter Vulcan cannon with 675 rounds mounted on the port side of the nose, and it can carry four AIM-7 Sparrow or AIM-54 Phoenix air-to-air missiles under the fuselage, PLUS a pylon under each inboard wing with additional Sparrow, Phoenix, Sidewinder, AMRAAM, or HARM missiles, *or* up to 14,500 pounds of Mk 80-series bombs.

When the Tomcat first appeared in the early 1970s, its design was revolutionary, not only because of the sweep wing configuration but also for the Heads-up Display (HUD) that projected critical information on the pilot's forward field of view and for the Hands-on-Throttle-and-Stick (HOTAS) that allowed the pilot to control radar modes, weapons selection, and so on with one hand *without* having to look down or inside the cockpit. In dogfights, this capability gave the edge to the F-14 pilot who, unlike his opponent, was able to keep his eyes outside the aircraft where they belonged.

In addition to its fighter role, the Tomcat has provisions to metamorphose into a reconnaissance aircraft with the attachment of the TARPS pod. As described in chapter 3, TARPS—and the new digital version, DI TARPS—allow the aircraft to conduct photo reconnaissance without degrading its performance in other roles. During Operation Desert

Storm in January and February 1991, F-14s flew 781 TARPS missions.

Several upgrades have been made to the Tomcat over the years, with the latest version being the F-14D. This multimission aircraft features new, more powerful F110-GE-400 engines (27,000 pounds of thrust per engine versus 20,900 pounds of thrust on the older TF-30P-414A engines), the new state-of-the-art multimode APG-71 radar system (which can identify noncooperative targets and perform advanced ground mapping in heavy weather), a digital flight-control system, night vision compatibility, an electronic warfare jamming system, and an infrared search-and-track system. Additionally, and perhaps most important, the F-14Ds were given the LANTIRN targeting system, which enables the RIO to deliver laser-guided bombs for precision strikes against ground targets. The Navy version of LANTIRN has a unique feature: It has a GPS/Inertial Navigation System capability, which means that it will be able to deliver the next generation of GPS-guided missiles and bombs, such as the Joint Direct Attack Munition (JDAM).

Unfortunately, the F-14 is nearing the end of its life, ironically, at a time when it finally has an engine and the avionics necessary to make it the fighter that aeronautical engineers originally envisioned. But due to the cost to operate and maintain them, the Navy intends to replace all Tomcats with F/A-18 Hornets by 2008.

Getting a Buzz

America's first strike fighter and now the backbone of naval aviation, the F/A-18 Hornet is designed to be both an attack aircraft *and* a fighter. It performs the same air-to-air and air-to-ground roles for the Navy and Marine Corps that the F-16 Fighting Falcon does for the Air Force. Hornets can be configured quickly to perform either fighter or attack roles, or both, through the types of weapons that are externally slung from the pylons. In its fighter role, the Hornet is used primarily as an escort to protect aircraft and ships from hostile aircraft. In its attack mode, it is used for force projection and combat air support, dropping bombs on enemy targets.

When the twin-engine Hornet became operational in 1983, it replaced the Navy's A-7 Corsair and A-6E Intruder attack aircraft, as well as the Marine Corps' F-4 Phantom, A-6E Intruder, A-4 Skyhawk, RF-4B Phantom, OA-4 Skyhawk, and OV-10 Bronco.

The introduction of the F/A-18 Hornet introduced pilots to a host of new technologies, including the "glass" cockpit, a cockpit composed only of computer screens that can be configured to display whatever information the pilot desires. Complementing this endeavor were second-generation HUD and HOTAS controls, which enabled the pilot to convert from "Attack" to "Fighter" mode with a flick of a switch. (The value of this feature was proven during Operation Desert Storm when two F/A-18s shot down a pair of Iraqi F-7 jets with a salvo of air-to-air missiles. The Hornets were loaded for a bombing mission at the time, but switched to the fighter mode, splashed the

The air operations room aboard the USS *George Washington* where the status of the carrier air wing's 70-plus aircraft are carefully monitored. If you look closely at the boards, you will note that most of the aircraft are conducting carquals (CQ). One aircraft is also running low on fuel (called "bingo" fuel status). Air Ops is located adjacent to the GW's CDC—combat direction center—directly beneath the flight deck. *S. F. Tomajczyk*

Joint Strike Fighter

Boeing Company

As the United States enters the 21st century, the Navy needs a highly survivable strike fighter to complement its new F/A-18 E/F "Super Hornet." Likewise, the Marine Corps needs to replace its aging fleet of AV-8B Harriers as its Short Takeoff and Vertical Landing (STOVL) aircraft. And the Air Force needs an air-to-ground strike aircraft to replace its F-16 Fighting Falcons and A-10 Warthogs, an aircraft that can also complement its new F-22A Raptor.

The answer to each of these dilemmas is the Joint Strike Fighter, a program started in the early 1990s to design an aircraft whose different variants could satisfy the needs of all three military services. Lockheed Martin and Boeing have both responded to the call,

and have built demonstration models of their aircraft, the X-35 and X-32, respectively. The Pentagon is scheduled to select the winning design in 2001.

The Boeing X-32 shown here, which resembles a cross between a modern F-22 Raptor and an ancient A-7 Corsair, is a stealthy, lightweight, and highly maneuverable aircraft capable of carrying more than 5,000 pounds of internal ordnance, such as the AIM-120 AMRAAM. The internal bay, which helps maintain the fighter's stealth when it is flying in heavily defended enemy airspace, could also accommodate the new, precision-guided JDAM and JSOW weapons. For additional firepower, the supersonic Boeing X-32 can also carry 12,000 pounds of external ordnance on four wing stations, as well as a gun mounted inside the chin inlet.

The pilot will have several tactical displays mounted on his helmet, which will allow him to have real-time situational awareness and targeting information. Additionally, aircraft sensors will provide the pilot with over-the-horizon detection of enemy threats, enabling him to replan the mission en route to the target.

The Navy's aircraft carrier variant, estimated to cost $31 to $38 million per unit, is 45 feet long with a 36-foot wingspan. This means that the fighter's blended, swept wings do not have to be folded like other aircraft to fit on the carrier's elevators or inside its crowded hangars. In fact, two JSF aircraft can fit side by side on a carrier elevator.

The Navy intends to transition from the F/A-18 Super Hornet to the Joint Strike Fighter as soon as it is demonstrated to be superior to the Super Hornet. Depending on the pace of the aircraft's progress, this transition could occur as early as 2008.

F-7s and then went on to finish their bombing mission.) And last, a fly-by-wire digital control system increased the responsiveness of the Hornet to the pilot's needs, especially in aerial combat.

In the past two decades, several models of the Hornet have been built, including the F/A-18A and C (both single seat) and the F/A-18B and D (both two-seat). The B model is used primarily for training, while the D model is the current Navy aircraft used by attack, tactical air control, forward air control, and reconnaissance squadrons.

The F/A-18 C and D models both have night-attack capability based on a forward-looking infrared sensor known as the Thermal Imaging Navigation Set, and they are equipped with an attack FLIR, a digital moving map, night vision goggles, and new cockpit displays. As with all Hornets, they have a six-barrel, 20-millimeter Vulcan cannon centered above the nose with 540 rounds for dogfights. In the fighter role, they carry either two AIM-9 Sidewinders and four AIM-7 Sparrow air-to-air missiles or six AIM-120 AMRAAMs. In the attack role, they carry two Sidewinders and up to 17,000 pounds of bombs, missiles, and rockets underwing (for example, HARM, SLAM, and Maverick). The Hornet is capable of tracking 10 targets simultaneously, displaying eight to the pilot.

For the delivery of precision-guided munitions like the Paveway LGB, the Hornet relies on the Nighthawk FLIR/Laser targeting pod, which is suspended from a fuselage station. Unlike the LANTIRN system found aboard the F-14 Tomcat, the Nighthawk is designed to be operated by just a single person, in this case the F/A-18 pilot. Once the pilot identifies the target, Nighthawk automatically tracks it and determines the release and delivery of the weapon.

At this writing, the Navy is about to introduce the latest models of the Hornet: the new E (single-seat) and F (two-seat) Super Hornets. These aircraft have a larger airframe, thicker and larger wings, a more powerful radar, improved engines that will provide 35 percent more thrust, larger leading-edge

F-14 Tomcat pilot Lieutenant Joe "Snacker" Dalton of the Blacklions (VF-213) demonstrates an air combat maneuver using "sticks" to show the relative positions of the engaged aircraft. On the board behind him is a bunch of "spaghetti," a line drawing of the maneuver from start to finish. Using such methods, followed by actual practice time in the sky, pilots learn how to conduct dozens of combat maneuvers, including the High Speed Yo-Yo, Lag Pursuit, and the Sandwich. The Blacklions are part of Carrier Air Wing 11. It was last deployed on the USS *Carl Vinson* (CVN-70). *S. F. Tomajczyk*

extensions to improve maneuverability, two additional weapon pylons, and a radar cross section that has been reduced to a mere 12.8 square feet. With a "buddy" fuel tank, they will also function as a tanker for in-flight refueling of other aircraft.

The Navy intends to acquire 535 Super Hornets; the first aircraft are expected to reach the

A test pilot fires an AIM-9 Sidewinder air-to-air missile from the new F/A-18F Super Hornet strike fighter. In an ideal world, F-14 and F/A-18 pilots go through five distinct phases when intercepting an enemy aircraft: detection of the enemy, closing with the aircraft, attacking, maneuver, and disengagement ("bug out"). More realistically, however, a pilot will detect the enemy and then shoot it down using a long-range missile. This simplifies the process to three steps: detection, attack, and disengagement. *U.S. Navy*

fleet in fiscal year 2000. The first squadrons will be located at Naval Air Station Lemore (California) and Oceana Naval Air Station (Virginia).

The Navy is also exploring the possibility of designing an electronic-attack version of the Super Hornet to initially assist and eventually replace the overworked EA-6B Prowler. Recent military operations in Bosnia have proven the need for more aircraft with radar-jamming capabilities. The aircraft, if built, would be able to do the Prowler's mission using systems currently in use—or under consideration for use—on the aircraft.

The Rest of the Air Wing

While much attention is given to a carrier's fighter and strike aircraft, it would not be able to do its mission without the support of other aircraft in the air wing. Jamming enemy SAM launchers and refueling the air wing's own fighters are two support roles essential to a successful mission.

Likewise, the Tomcats and Hornets are handicapped when it comes to conducting other types of missions that a CVBG needs to protect itself from enemy attack and to successfully fight a battle. Antisubmarine warfare is a good example.

So let's take a brief look at the rest of the carrier air wing and see how the aircraft fit into the battle group:

SH-60 Seahawk—The primary mission of the Seahawk is antisubmarine warfare (ASW). It is outfitted with sonobuoys and a retractable magnetic-anomaly detector (MAD) sensor to detect submerged submarines. It is also armed with torpedoes. The LAMPS III–equipped Seahawk increases the ASW capabilities of surface ships. (See chapter 6.) Other missions for the Seahawk include search-and-rescue, vertical replenishment, and ship surveillance and targeting. Aboard an aircraft carrier, a Seahawk serves as "Plane Guard" when aircraft are launched or recovered. It is always the first aircraft to become airborne; it is positioned near the carrier to rescue aircrew if their plane crashes.

E-2C Hawkeye—Known as the "Hummer," the Hawkeye is an airborne early-warning aircraft designed to provide a CVBG with over-the-horizon surveillance. It also serves as an air controller, directing fighters against hostile targets. The turboprop aircraft's most notable feature is a 24-foot-diameter saucer-like UHF radome ("frisbee") perched on a pylon above the fuselage that sweeps all points of the compass. Rotating freely in the airstream at 6 revolutions per minute, the 2,000-pound radome can see targets up to 300 miles away (150 miles for small targets such as cruise missiles) when at an altitude of 30,000 feet. The system is capable of monitoring 3 million cubic miles of airspace in one 10-second scan. The Hawkeye can simultaneously track some 250 bogeys and guide up to 30 interceptor aircraft to various targets. (Note: The newer and more powerful APS-145 radar can track up to 2,000 targets while controlling 20 interceptor aircraft.) Its passive detection system can detect enemy radar up to 600 miles away.

Speed and maneuverability are everything in a dogfight. In this spectacular photo, an F/A-18 Hornet assigned to VF-151 is shown breaking the sound barrier in July 1999. VF-151 was deployed with the USS *Constellation* (CV-64) battle group at the time. *U.S. Navy*

The beauty of the Hawkeye is that fighters like the F-14 Tomcat can "dump" its radar system's target information on up to 24 aircraft to the Hawkeye, permitting the fighter to acquire another two dozen targets.

Hawkeyes are always the first fixed-wing aircraft to be launched from the carrier's flight deck (and the last to recover). To facilitate this, they are parked next to the island so they can get to the catapult as quickly as possible. The pilot usually flies a zigzag pattern at low altitude to prevent an enemy AEW aircraft from detecting his departure and locating the aircraft carrier.

The plane crew consists of a pilot, co-pilot, CIC officer, air controller, and a radar operator/technician. The latter three are referred to as "Moles" since they work in the dark confines of the aircraft's fuselage.

Air Intercept Missiles

AIM-7 Sparrow (F-14, F/A-18): A highly maneuverable radar-guided missile with a 90-pound blast fragmentation warhead with proximity fuse. It is capable of attacking aircraft and missiles in any direction. Guidance: Semi-active on continuous wave or pulsed Doppler radar energy. Speed: Mach 3.5 to Mach 4. Range: 60-plus miles.

AIM-9M Sidewinder (F-14, F/A-18, AV-8B, AH-1W): A fire-and-forget, heat-seeking, short-range missile with a 20.8-pound blast fragmentation warhead. It is commonly used for fleet air defense and short-range dogfights. Guidance: Solid state, infrared passive homing and an active optical target detector. Speed: Mach 2.5. Range: 10-plus miles.

AIM-9X (F/A-18): The next generation of the Sidewinder missile. The short-range missile is designed to turn almost 90 degrees from the launching aircraft to lock on to targets. It features an enhanced imaging infrared seeker that can detect targets beyond human sight, an improved warhead/fuse, and it will be redesigned to reduce drag. The AIM-9X normally acquires its targets by using its own seeker, but it also can use advanced cueing modes linked to the aircraft's radar or by a helmet-mounted sight worn by the pilot. With the helmet-mounted sight, a pilot need only look at his target and fire. First deliveries are expected to take place in late 2001. Guidance: midwave, infrared focal plane array. Speed: Classified. Range: Classified.

AIM-54 Phoenix (F-14): A sophisticated, long-range missile with a 135-pound proximity-fuse, high explosive, controlled-fragmentation warhead. The Phoenix, which was specifically developed for long-range air defense of CVBGs, is carried in clusters of up to six missiles aboard the F-14. It has a look-down capability out to 150 miles and is backed-up with an infrared tracker to assist in positive target identification. Guidance: Semi-active during the cruise phase, with active radar homing during the terminal phase. Speed: 3,000 miles per hour. Range: 125-plus miles.

AIM-120 AMRAAM (F-14, F/A-18): A medium-range, fire-and-forget tactical missile with a 50-pound blast fragmentation, high explosive warhead. This missile replaces the AIM-7 Sparrow and is faster, smaller, and lighter, and has improved capabilities against low-altitude targets. Guidance: Midcourse inertial reference system with active radar terminal homing. Speed: Mach 4. Range: 30 to 45 miles.

Air-to-Ground Missiles

AGM-65F Maverick (F/A-18, AV-8B): A laser-guided tactical missile with a 300-pound penetrating warhead designed for close air support. Two types of warhead are used: one with a contact fuse in the nose; the other is a heavyweight warhead with a delayed fuse, which penetrates the target before exploding. The Maverick is used against armor, air defenses, ships, vehicles, and fuel storage facilities. Guidance: Infrared homing. Speed: Supersonic. Range: 17-plus miles.

AGM-84D Harpoon (F-14, F/A-18, P-3, S-3B): A long-range, sea-skimming antiship cruise missile. Guidance: Radar altimeter with active radar terminal homing. Speed: Mach 0.85. Range: 60-plus miles.

AGM-84E SLAM (F/A-18): An infrared-seeking variant of the Harpoon cruise missile used for long-range precision strikes against land targets. It has a 488-pound penetration, high explosive blast warhead. SLAM (Standoff Land-Attack Missile) allows the pilot to make in-flight guidance corrections base on infrared video images transmitted by the missile. Guidance: Inertial navigation with GPS with imaging infrared seeker for terminal guidance. Speed: Mach 0.85. Range: 60-plus miles.

SLAM-ER (F/A-18): A new long-range, precision land-attack cruise missile that can find targets in cluttered environments. An upgraded version of the

SLAM, SLAM-ER (Standoff Land-Attack Missile, Expanded Response) is hardened against most countermeasures and its titanium warhead has penetration capability. It entered service in 1999. Guidance: GPS/INS with an infrared seeker for terminal guidance. A datalink allows the pilot to retarget the impact point during the last 5 miles. Speed: High subsonic. Range: 150-plus miles.

AGM-88 HARM (F-14, F/A-18, EA-6B): A tactical missile with a 150-pound blast fragmentation, proximity-fuse warhead designed to seek out and destroy enemy radar-equipped air defense systems, such as SAM launchers. The missile homes in on any radiating target regardless of its angle from the launching aircraft. HARM (High-speed, Anti-Radiation Missile) is often used with the Tactical Air Launched Decoy, a decoy that tricks SAM sites into turning on their radar systems. Guidance: Passive radar homing system that targets radar emissions. Speed: Mach 2. Range: 80-plus miles.

AGM-114 Hellfire (AH-1J, AH-1W): A supersonic, fire-and-forget anti-armor, laser-guided missile. While in flight, the Hellfire detects laser radiation (ground or airborne based) that illuminates a target. It locks on and homes in on the target, destroying it with a 20-pound high explosive, hollow charge warhead. A third generation of four advanced Hellfire missile designs (AGMS, Air-to-Ground Missile System) is used by the AH-1W Super Cobra attack helicopter. Guidance: Semi-active laser homing. Speed: Mach 1.17. Range: 3-plus miles.

AGM-122 Sidearm (AV-8B, AH-1J): A supersonic, antiradar missile with a 10-pound, high-explosive blast fragmentation warhead that is derived from the AIM-9C Sidewinder. It is used to attack ground-based, air-defense weapons at short range. Guidance: Radar homing plus electro-optical target detection. Speed: Mach 2.3. Range: 10 miles.

AGM-123A Skipper II (F/A-18): A laser-guided bomb that uses the laser-guidance and control sections from the unpowered Paveway II LGB, along with the 1,000-pound, high explosive warhead from a Mk-83 GP bomb and a rocket engine similar to the one used by the AGM-45A Shrike guided missile. Guidance: Laser-guidance seeker. Speed: Transonic. Range: 10 miles.

AGM-142 HAVE NAP (F/A-18): A medium-range, guided stand-off missile with a 1,975-pound, high explosive warhead. Guidance: Inertial system with either an electro-optical or imaging infrared terminal guidance seeker. Speed: Subsonic. Range: 50 miles.

Miscellaneous

JDAM (F-14, F/A-18, AV-8B, JSF): JDAM is essentially a guidance kit strapped on to one of three conventional bombs: the Mk-83 (1,000-pound), Mk-84 (2,000-pound), or BLU-109 penetrating warhead (2,000-pound). The kit consists of a GPS guidance system and control fins. After the bomb is dropped by the launch aircraft, JDAM takes its guidance from GPS satellites, enabling it to guide the bomb to within 40 feet of the target. JDAM (Joint Direct Attack Munition) is identified by two military designations: GBU-31 (the 1,000-pound Mk 83 bomb) and GBU-32 (the 2,000-pound Mk 84 or the BLU-109 bomb). JDAM entered military service in 1999. Guidance: INS/GPS. Range: 27-plus miles.

AGM-154 JSOW (F/A-18, JSF): A follow-on variant of the JDAM that will have a solid-propellant rocket, folding wings, and enhanced guidance systems. It will carry either a 500-pound Mk-82 HE warhead or the BLU-108 sensor fused, anti-armor submunitions warhead. JSOW stands for Joint Stand-Off Weapon. The initial model (AGM-154A) is operational with the fleet and was deployed to the 1997 Iraq crisis. Guidance: INS/GPS. Speed: Classified. Range: Classified.

Steam from the catapult surrounds a "BB Stacker" as he gives a thumbs-up after checking a joint direct attack munitions (JDAM) attached to an F/A-18C Hornet before it launches from the USS *Kitty Hawk* (CV-63). JDAM is a state-of-the-art weapon that uses a GPS-aided inertial navigation system to guide its 1,000- or 2,000-pound warhead to the target. *U.S. Navy*

The Hawkeye can remain on station for six hours, 200 miles from the aircraft carrier.

EA-6B Prowler—The Prowler is a tactical electronic-warfare aircraft that provides an umbrella of protection for strike aircraft and the CVBG against hostile radar. The aircraft is heavily equipped with EW transmitters to jam enemy radar, data links, and communications. This makes it virtually impossible for the enemy to launch anti-aircraft/antiship, radar-guided missiles. The primary receiver antennas are located in a fairing on top of the aircraft's tail (the "football"), which provides all-around, long-distance coverage of enemy emitters. The data received by these antennas are processed by an onboard computer, which automatically fine-tunes the radiated jamming power to match that of the threat and then aims it directly at the enemy source.

The jammers themselves are housed inside self-powered pods suspended from wing pylons and the fuselage. The Prowler can carry up to five pods, each with two jamming transmitters. Each pod is designed to cover up to seven different radio frequency bands and can simultaneously jam any two.

Modifications were made to the Prowler, enabling

it to carry four high-speed, antiradiation missiles so that when an enemy SAM launcher is discovered, it can be immediately destroyed.

The value of the Prowler has been proven time and again. During the 1991 Gulf War, for instance, Prowlers flew more than 1,600 missions, successfully jamming Iraqi EW and command, control, and communications capabilities and destroying several radar sites.

During Operation Allied Force in 1999, Prowlers escorted combat air patrols over Kosovo, as well as all Air Force F-117 and B-2 stealth aircraft that flew on missions. The need for Air Force escorts was brought about by the downing of an F-117 Nighthawk by Yugoslav air defense forces. (Note: The Air Force had retired its version of the Prowler, the EF-111 Raven, after the Gulf War.) The Kosovo conflict severely overburdened the Prowlers, with some squadrons flying six-hour missions daily. This has since caused the Navy and the Pentagon to scramble to either acquire more Prowlers or build a new EW aircraft (meaning, the F/A-18G) to respond to future conflicts.

The EA-6B Prowler has an aircrew of four: the pilot plus three electronic countermeasures operators, seated abreast in pairs and in tandem. In times of conflict, a language expert is often assigned as a naval flight officer aboard the Prowler to operate communications intelligence equipment.

S-3B Viking—The Viking is the CVBG's primary antisubmarine warfare aircraft that is designed to seek out and destroy enemy submarines and provide surveillance of surface ships. It typically operates in the battle group's mid- to outer-ASW zones searching for hostile threats, with the SH-60 Seahawk LAMPS III in support. (See chapter 6.) The Viking can be armed with the Mk-46 homing torpedo, Mk-54 depth charges, Mk-82 bombs, Mk-53 mines, and the AGM-84 Harpoon antiship cruise missile.

In addition to its ASW role, the S-3B Viking serves as an in-flight refueler to other aircraft. It carries a two-pod "buddy" refueling system that enables the F-14, F/A-18, and other carrier-based aircraft to refuel.

Naval Air Combat

When an aircraft carrier battle group is at sea, it establishes a series of defensive umbrellas over it to protect itself from enemy air attack, whether by plane or missile. Each of these umbrellas differs in size and the types of weapons used to counterattack a hostile force.

The innermost umbrella, which is usually centered on the carrier, is known as the "point missile defense zone." It has a radius of about 5 miles, and all the ships positioned within it use their guns, short-range missiles, and 20-millimeter Phalanx CIWS (Close-In Weapon System) to defend themselves. Theoretically, no enemy should ever get this close, but then again, we don't live in a theoretical world.

The outer two umbrellas are the area missile defense zone (which extends 35 miles beyond the innermost zone) and the aircraft defense zone (which extends 60 miles beyond the middle zone). These are generally defended by medium-range missiles fired from surface warships, which have been carefully positioned within the umbrella based on the range of their missiles. The outer periphery of the umbrella is patrolled by heavily armed fighter aircraft.

As the CVBG moves forward, its 100-mile-radius air-defense umbrella travels with it, constantly changing its shape and force allocation depending on perceived and real enemy threats. The entire defensive airspace is controlled by the air combat commander, who is aboard the Redcrown warship. Using information from the AEGIS combat system as well as from the E-2C Hawkeye and CAP fighters, Redcrown orchestrates any response required to protect the CVBG from attack.

As mentioned earlier, one of the more difficult things to do is properly identify friendly aircraft. This is particularly true when an F-14 Tomcat or F/A-18 Hornet needs to return to the carrier for rearming or refueling. Redcrown cannot allow it to come anywhere near the carrier or the inner zone until it is identified. Fortunately, all U.S. and NATO planes are equipped with an IFF—Identification, Friend or Foe—

In a defensive move to thwart an incoming heat-seeking missile, an F/A-18C Hornet from strike fighter squadron 146 expends a series of hot flares. This was done over the Pacific Ocean during a training exercise designed to prepare the squadron for its next deployment aboard the USS *John C. Stennis* (CVN-74). Several times a week, U.S. and allied aircraft launch air strikes against Iraqi targets in retaliation for anti-aircraft fire and radar illumination of allied aircraft patrolling the no-fly zones over northern and southern Iraq. During the first nine months of 1999, the United States and Britain flew 10,000 sorties and dropped 1,000 bombs and missiles at 400 targets in Iraq. This ongoing and dangerous campaign is what pilots face when their carrier air wing deploys to the Persian Gulf, which is why training is ongoing and intense. *U.S. Navy*

transponder that sends out a signal identifying it as a friendly aircraft. Unfortunately, it can also fail.

When this occurs, or when an unidentified aircraft approaches the CVBG's airspace, Redcrown orders a CAP to intercept and clearly identify the target. This is often done more than 100 miles from the carrier, giving Redcrown several minutes to decide on a course of action should the target prove to be hostile. For instance, Redcrown can order escort surface warships to prepare to shoot down the target with their missiles. Or it can vector another CAP to intercept the target. Or, if need be, it can launch more fighter aircraft from the carrier flight deck.

Understandably, the Redcrown CIC becomes quite tense in these situations.

For the pilots, as much as they enthusiastically jest about wanting to get into a dogfight with the enemy, they know deep inside that it is anything but a joking matter. Since the day they first stepped foot inside NAS Pensacola to become a naval aviator, they have been taught how dangerous aerial combat is. They learn, for instance, that most combat engagements occur at long distance with high-speed missiles and are over within seconds. If they are not alert, they will likely be shot down before ever seeing the enemy.

They also learn that rate-of-turn is more important than radius-of-turn. So even if you are flying a "Speed of Heat" fighter that can turn on a dime, if it takes you longer to make that turn than your opponent, you're toast. No ifs, ands, or buts about it.

And they learn that it is vitally important to outlast your opponent in a dogfight. As aircraft speeds and maneuverability have increased, the time actually spent in a dogfight has dramatically fallen. Furthermore, a dogfight requires the use of the afterburner, which consumes fuel like a starved, ferocious lion. All this boils down to the fact that a pilot only has so many maneuvers he can make during a dogfight before it's time to disengage. Pilots know that "he who leaves first, loses," because the plane that bugs-out first is usually low on fuel and, hence, unable to maneuver from a missile shot.

Complicating all this are other inherent dangers associated with aerial combat. For instance, a pilot is subject to blackout if he pulls too many Gs when yanking and banking his plane to avoid or chase the enemy. As the G-forces increase, more blood is drained away from his head. At first, he loses his color perception and his vision takes on the appearance of a black-and-white movie. This is followed by loss of peripheral vision, the tunnel-vision effect, and, finally, complete loss of sight. The degree to which G-forces adversely affect a pilot depends on his physical well-being. "Grayout" can begin as early as 3 Gs or as high as 8 Gs for the same pilot on different days.

Pilots can also lose situational awareness of the ever-changing, three-dimensional air battle going on around them. If they forget who is where and doing what, they are in deep trouble.

For these and many other reasons, pilots enter a dogfight with a healthy respect for their opponent and do everything they can to aggressively win the battle as quickly as they can, even if it means using a long-range missile. There's no disgrace in returning to the flight deck alive if you splashed the enemy at 30 miles. No one says you have to be filled with holes.

Chapter 5

Surface Warfare
Slugging It Out

Throughout history, the basic premise of a so-called "naval engagement" was for opposing warships to line up opposite each other and fire hundreds of shells at each other until one—or both—sank or surrendered. Recognizing that it was not healthy for ships to be too close to one another, navies began developing technologies to allow them to shoot at enemy ships from farther away. Doing so gave them an edge: They could sink a ship before it could react and fire back. This is the premise of surface warfare, and the trend to attack and sink ships at stand-off distances continues.

Today, at the dawn of the twenty-first century, the U.S. Navy finds itself capable of launching attacks against enemy forces positioned well over the horizon—in some cases, hundreds of miles away. The targets include not only warships but, increasingly, important land-based targets as well, such as military airfields, command posts, and supply depots. This is exemplified by American military actions conducted during Operations Desert Storm, Desert Fox, and Allied Force. In all of these major conflicts, CVBGs were able to successfully attack targets deep

In more than 80 percent of the times when the world was faced with international violence, the United States has responded with one or more carrier battle groups.

Department of the Navy

inside the borders of the hostile nation.

It is this power projection capability that earns a battle group the respect of military forces around the world. Ironically, it is also this stand-off attack capability that keeps a battle group commander leery of other naval fleets he encounters when deployed at sea. He knows they are constantly developing ways to attack his warships from greater distances. In the back of his mind is always the burning question: *Is this the day?*

The key to winning a naval engagement is for a battle group to detect and properly identify enemy warships first, before they do. To this end, the CVBG relies on a plethora of assets—radar, surveillance aircraft, SIGINT, submarines, satellites, picket ships—to determine where the hostile fleet is located, where it is heading, and what its intentions are. A battle group routinely establishes a huge zone around it for the purpose of extending a watchful eye over the horizon, using primarily ships and aircraft, thereby buying time for it to decide on an appropriate response.

As the CVBG steams through the sea, the main body changes course every so often to reduce the

A test launch of the vertical launch system (VLS) aboard a Ticonderoga-class guided-missile cruiser that is equipped with the powerful AEGIS combat system. AEGIS was developed to counter possible saturation missile attacks launched by the Soviet Union. Conventional, rotating radar systems were found to be too slow to handle such an attack, so AEGIS was born. Four planar SPY-1 antennas were mounted to the corners of the superstructure, each covering a 45-degree sector. The SPY-1 arrays hunt for predetermined target descriptions. The system then evaluates, arranges in sequence of threat, and finally engages (automatically or in manual override) the target with one of the ship's weapon systems. The VLS is often selected since it is capable of firing any one of three types of missiles: the BGM-109 Tomahawk, RIM-66 Standard, and the RUM-139 Vertical Launch ASROC. *U.S. Navy*

The Arleigh Burke–class destroyer USS *Benfold* (DDG-65) fires its 5-inch gun during a training exercise off the southern coast of California. The gun provides warships with accurate naval gunfire against surface, air, and shore targets. *U.S. Navy*

threat posed by hostile submarines. Meanwhile, outlying escorts constantly and aggressively patrol sectors 60 to 75 square miles, guarding the main body from attack while searching over the horizon for the subtlest sign of enemy warships.

It stands to reason that the larger the zone radius, the sooner a battle group is able to detect potential trouble. Yet, at some point there is a distinct trade-off in safety, where the zone becomes so large that a CVBG's escorts are spread out too much, allowing enemy submarines and small warships an opportunity to slip through the cracks. Hence, a battle group commander must carefully position his destroyers, cruisers, and frigates in such a manner to "see" over the horizon without jeopardizing the safety of the aircraft carrier. In the end, their deployment is determined largely by the capabilities of their detection and weapons systems.

Contrary to popular belief, the zone established around a CVBG is not equi-distant from the center. The zone is a flexible creature, constantly changing in size and shape to accommodate emerging situations. As a rule of thumb, though, most zones in open ocean have a diameter of about 250 miles, with the majority of warships positioned in those areas of the zone that face the threat, whether real or perceived.

For example, if a battle group is steaming 200 miles off the coast of a hostile nation, it will usually organize itself so that several layers of warships are between the aircraft carrier and the shore—often the direction of the greatest threat—and an escort is positioned far ahead of the CVBG to detect oncoming hostile ships. A fewer number of warships are located to the seaward side of the carrier. As for lightly armed ships, such as a replenishment vessel, they are placed the farthest away from the coast to avoid being targeted by antiship cruise missiles or enemy warships.

Another misperception is that the zone must focus on the aircraft carrier. If the carrier were always placed at the center of a zone, the enemy would know exactly where to launch an attack. To confuse the enemy, a battle group often divides itself into several subgroups so that it is unclear which contains the high-value ships. (Keep in mind that the first contact an enemy force has with a CVBG is nearly always with its radar systems, not the human eye. It is difficult by looking solely at a radar scope to determine what a "blip" actually represents.) In the war of deception, battle groups have even been known to place a fleet oiler or fast combat support ship (which have radar signatures similar to those of an aircraft carrier) in areas of the zone where the carrier might be expected to be located. This tactic really gets the enemy cross-eyed.

Naval Armada

The CVBG has three types of surface warships at its disposal to wage war on the high seas: destroyers, cruisers, and frigates. A modern 10-ship battle group typically heads to sea with a cruiser-destroyer group comprised of two guided-missile cruisers (CG), two guided-missile destroyers (DDG), and one destroyer (DD). Two guided-missile frigates (FFG) are also included. The frigates and destroyer are generally used for antisubmarine warfare, while the guided-missile destroyers and cruisers are multimission surface combatants capable of conducting anti-air warfare and long-range strike.

Guided-missile cruiser—These warships serve as multimission surface combatants and are capable of screening battle groups and amphibious forces. They can also operate independently or as a flagship of surface action groups. All cruisers are armed with antiaircraft missiles and all have antisubmarine warfare capabilities. At this writing there is only one class of CG-designated cruiser in service, the Ticonderoga-class (CG 47-73).

Measuring 567 feet long and displacing up to 9,600 tons fully loaded, the 27 "Ticos" of this class can travel in excess of 30 knots and have a range of 6,600 miles when steaming at 20 knots. The cruisers are heavily armed with eight Harpoon antiship missiles and two 61-cell vertical launch systems (VLS), which can launch Tomahawk cruise missiles, Vertical ASROC antisubmarine rockets, and Standard anti-aircraft missiles. Additionally, they carry two Mk-45 5-inch guns, two 20-millimeter Phalanx "gatling" guns for point defense, and six 12.75-inch torpedo tubes.

The ships, which cost $1 billion apiece, are equipped with the AEGIS combat system, various electronic warfare systems, and a variety of sonar and radar. The cruisers also carry two SH-60B Seahawk LAMPS III antisubmarine helicopters. By using their hull-mounted sonar, an acoustic array sonar towed behind the ship, and the SH-60B, the Ticos can detect and attack enemy submarines more than 100 miles away.

Ticos are known to be in the midst of things when trouble arises; they love to fight. During the 1991 Gulf War, for example, seven Ticos fired 105 Tomahawk missiles against Iraqi targets, 36 percent of all Tomahawks fired during the war.

The Navy intends to upgrade the aging Ticos with a host of new systems and capabilities by 2005. Beginning in 2002, the cruisers will be upgraded to provide theater missile defense using the improved version of the Standard anti-air missile (SM-3), and they will be outfitted with the Land-Attack Standard Missile (LASM) and the Extended Range Guided Munition (ERGM).

A RIM-7P Sea Sparrow surface-to-air missile is fired from an Mk-29 guided-missile launching system aboard the USS *George Washington*. This particular launcher is located next to the LSO platform. Aircraft carriers, which are lightly armed, rely on their force of better-armed escorts—destroyers and cruisers—for protection from enemy attack. *U.S. Navy*

Guided-missile destroyer—These warships perform a variety of missions, including antisubmarine warfare, anti-air warfare, and antisurface warfare. With the decommissioning of the last Kidd-class DDG in 1999, there is only one class of DDG remaining in service, the Arleigh Burke class (DDG 51-88).

Arguably the most powerful surface combatant ever put to sea, the 504-foot-long Arleigh Burke destroyers, which displace 8,300 tons fully loaded, are intended to complement AEGIS cruisers in the air/missile-defense of carrier battle groups and to replace existing DDGs and CGs as escorts. They derive their combat capability from the AEGIS combat system and the SPY-1D, a powerful, multifunction, phased-array radar, which can "see" enemy targets as far away as 250 miles. The flat radar antennas are located at the four corners of the superstructure block, angled at 45 degrees.

The ships are armed with a 90-cell VLS (29 forward, 61 aft) for Standard, Tomahawk, and Vertical ASROC missiles, plus two four-tube Harpoon antiship missile launchers, one Mk-45 5-inch gun, two Phalanx 20-millimeter CIWSes, and six 12.75-inch torpedo tubes. The destroyers are equipped with a variety of radar and sonar systems, including the TACTAS towed-sonar array and bow-mounted sonar.

Three Arleigh Burke–class destroyers, the *Higgins* (DDG-76), *Donald Cook* (DDG-75), and USS *Mahan* (DDG-72), at sea in late 1998. This class of destroyer features steel superstructures, which provide increased resistance to fragments, fire damage, blast overpressure, and nuclear electromagnetic pulse. In addition, the destroyers have 130 tons of bulletproof Kevlar armor plating to protect vital areas of the ship, and have an overpressure system to allow them to operate in NBC-contaminated environments. To further ensure survivability, the ships' combat information center is located within the hull, surrounded by passageways. Also, the data-processing architecture is distributed to ensure that the ships' weaponry cannot be disabled by a single hit, and the sonar room is placed well forward away from the CIC. *Bath Iron Works*

The Arleigh Burke class was designed from the start for stealth and survivability. For example, the angled superstructure and funnels significantly lower its radar cross section over other destroyer classes.

As for survivability, these warships are the first since World War II to have steel superstructures, which provide increased resistance to fragments, fire

damage, blast overpressure, and nuclear electromagnetic pulse. In addition, they have 130 tons of bulletproof Kevlar armor plating to protect vital areas of the ship and have an overpressure system to allow them to operate in environments contaminated by nuclear, biological, or chemical warfare.

Destroyer—Commissioned between 1975 and 1983, the Spruance class was constructed as specialized antisubmarine warfare vessels; however, they were eventually equipped for anti-air and land-attack roles with the addition of the Tomahawk missile. These destroyers have an overall length of 563 feet and displace 8,040 tons fully loaded. They are armed with one eight-tube Sea Sparrow launcher for limited air/missile-defense capability, two launchers for the Harpoon antiship missile (four missiles to each launcher), a 61-cell VLS for the Tomahawk or Vertical ASROC missiles, two Mk-45 5-inch guns, two 20-millimeter Phalanx CIWSes, and six 12.75-inch torpedo tubes. The ships also carry two SH-60B Seahawk LAMPS III antisubmarine helicopters.

Five destroyers of the Spruance class—the Caron, Fife, Leftwich, Foster, and Spruance—launched 112 Tomahawk missiles at Iraqi targets during the 1991 Gulf War. In fact, the USS *Paul F. Foster* fired the opening salvo of the Gulf War on January 17, 1991. The USS *Fife* launched 60 Tomahawk missiles.

Frigate—Although frigates have traditionally provided ASW protection, the Oliver Hazard Perry class (FFG 7-61) offers a limited anti-air warfare defense to amphibious and replenishment groups. These sturdy vessels have an overall length of 445 feet and displace 3,658 tons fully loaded. Their weapon systems include a launcher for the Standard surface-to-air missile or the Harpoon anti-ship missile, an Oto Melara Mk-75 76-millimeter dual purpose gun, a 20-millimeter Phalanx CIWS, and two triple launchers for the 12.75-inch torpedo. The ships also carry two SH-60B LAMPS III antisubmarine helicopters.

Although these frigates lack hull-mounted active/passive sonar and ASROC launchers, they do have towed sonar arrays, electronic warfare systems, and ASW helicopters to make up for it.

During the 1991 Gulf War, several frigates operated U.S. Army OH-58 special operations helicopters as well as their own ASW helicopters against Iraqi forces. Perhaps the best-known frigate was the USS *Stark,* which was struck by two Exocet cruise missiles while operating in the Persian Gulf. She was decommissioned in 1999.

The Vertical Launch System

As you read through the descriptions of these warships, you cannot help but notice that several weapon systems are repeated. That is for a good reason: The systems work, and they work lethally well. How the weapons are deployed, and in what number, is generally what separates one type of surface combatant from another. For instance, ships whose primary role is ASW have fewer air-defense weapons but more ASW capabilities.

The Navy's most advanced warships are equipped with the Vertical Launch System (VLS), which enables a ship to vertically store several different missile types that are ready for instantaneous use in combat. Each ship has anywhere from 60 to 120 VLS cells.

When a CVBG deploys overseas, it brings with it a certain number of VLS cells that make up a portion of the firepower a battle group commander has at his disposal. According to the Navy, a major regional contingency requires at least 3,500 VLS cells to be present. At any given time, there are about 1,500 VLS cells deployed around the world on U.S. warships; a typical 10-ship CVBG has a combined total of 495 VLS cells.

The VLS was designed to allow a warship to carry more missiles than what the traditional armored "box" launch system allowed. The VLS is actually embedded into the ship's hull forward of the superstructure or aft so that the hatches at the top of the tubes (or "cells") are nearly flush with the main deck. The cells are arranged to store either 29 or 61 missiles. (By comparison, two armored box launchers that

The business end of the heavily armed, guided-missile cruiser USS *Cape St. George* (CG-71). In addition to two 5-inch guns (one of which is shown here), she has two 61-cell VLS launchers filled with missiles, eight Harpoon antiship missiles, six torpedo tubes, and two Phalanx CIWSes. One of the VLS launchers can be seen in this photo on the deck directly behind the gun. The square-shaped hatches open when the missile is fired. The USS *Cape St. George* is one of the first warships in the Navy outfitted with the revolutionary Cooperative Engagement Capability (CEC). CEC pushes the engagement zone over the horizon, by connecting ships, aircraft, and land stations into a single network where information from their radar and other sensors is instantaneously shared with one another. CEC widens and clarifies the picture they all have of the battlespace. For the USS *Cape St. George,* this means she can exchange real-time, fire-control quality track data with other CEC-equipped ships. This capability enables, for instance, a ship to use another's fire control data to shoot down a missile or plane. *S. F. Tomajczyk*

DD-21 Land-Attack Destroyer

Illustration courtesy of United Defense

There is an axiom that states, "What goes around, comes around." Where the gun-bristling warships of old are concerned, it appears that they are about to be resurrected in the form of the DD-21 Land-Attack Destroyer, the Navy's next generation of guided-missile destroyer. The DD-21, which is presently being designed by two separate teams, is anticipated to have a radical outward appearance due to the stealthy features stipulated by the Navy, plus a slew of weapon systems.

Guns will be a major component of the DD-21, with the Navy recently deciding on a single-barrel, 155-millimeter advanced gun system (AGS). The AGS will be capable of striking targets with high accuracy at 100-mile ranges—far greater than today's 15-mile range. The 155-millimeter shells will be able to penetrate armor and destroy tanks, thereby providing inland combat troops with tremendous gunfire support. The AGS will fire 12 rounds per minute and will have a 600- to 750-round magazine capacity.

Another shell being designed for the 155-millimeter gun is the extended range guided munition (ERGM) rocket shell. The ERGM will use GPS satellites to "fly" to the intended target area 40 to 65 miles away, where it will release a canister of antipersonnel or antimateriel submunitions at an altitude of 750 to 1,200 feet above the ground. A prototype of the ERGM, albeit a smaller version weighing-in at only 100 pounds, is intended to be deployed on several Arleigh Burke–class destroyers and tested using their 5-inch guns. Testing will begin in 2002.

Supplementing the AGS, which is already being lauded as the "King of the Battlefield," will be the DD-21's several hundred missiles, including the Tactical Tomahawk and the still-evolving Advanced Land-Attack Missile (ALAM).

The Navy envisions buying 32 DD-21s at a total cost of up to $25 billion. Their initial deployment is scheduled for 2008. In early 1999, the Navy reactivated its stealth test ship, the *Sea Shadow*. It will be used to test various concepts and technologies that are slated to be incorporated not only into the DD-21 but also into a heavily armed 2,000-ton stealth warship known as the "Street Fighter." The Street Fighter is intended to complement the DD-21 and operate in waters off enemy coastlines.

occupy about the same amount of space as a 61-cell VLS can only store eight Tomahawk missiles.) Ticonderoga-class guided-missile cruisers have two 61-cell VLS aboard, while the new Arleigh Burke-class guided-missile destroyers have a 90-cell VLS (29 cells forward and 61 cells aft). Twenty-four ships of the Spruance class have a 61-cell VLS installed, replacing the ASROC launcher.

The Vertical Launch System is designed to launch any one of three types of missiles: the BGM-109 Tomahawk, RIM-66 Standard, and the RUM-139 Vertical Launch ASROC.

Tomahawk—The Tomahawk is the Navy's premiere long-range, subsonic (550-mile-per-hour) cruise missile, designed to be launched from surface warships and submarines against enemy ships and land targets. After being launched, a solid propellant rocket booster propels the missile until a small turbofan engine takes over for the cruise portion of the flight. The Tomahawk is highly survivable because of its small radar cross section and its ability to fly at low altitudes following an evasive flight path.

There are two types of Tomahawks in use with the Navy: one for land attacks (TLAM) and the other for surface ships (TASM). The Block II TLAM version uses a terrain comparison and digital-matching guidance system. As the missile flies toward its target—up to 610 miles away—it uses an internal, digitized computer map to determine exactly where it is by comparing the surrounding terrain with the map. If necessary, the missile can adjust its bearing to get back on the correct course.

The current Block III TLAM adds Global Positioning Satellite guidance capability to the terrain comparison and digital-matching efforts. This means that the missile receives constant navigation data from the Defense Department's 24 GPS satellites. The result is extreme accuracy: The missile remains roughly within 16 feet of its intended flight path.

As for the Tomahawk Anti-Ship Missile (TASM), its guidance system allows the missile to literally skim the ocean's surface to avoid being detected by enemy radar. At a predetermined distance from the target ship, the TASM begins an active radar search to acquire and then home in on the ship. It has a 220-mile range and carries a warhead packed with 1,000 pounds of high explosive. The Navy has removed TASM from its surface ships and placed them in storage for possible conversion into a more advanced weapon system. In its place, ships rely on the Harpoon anti-ship missile.

The Tomahawk is a versatile cruise missile, capable of carrying both nuclear (W80) and conventional warheads, as well as dispense bomblets (as many as 168 armor-piercing, fragmentation, or incendiary bomblets) over a target area, such as an airport runway. The nuclear version of the Tomahawk (TLAM-N) has a range of 1,050 miles.

There is yet another version of the Tomahawk: a quasi-electronic warfare variant that is filled with thousands of carbon spools. When the warhead explodes over an electric power plant, the spools unwind and the microscopic fibers fall onto the power lines and transformers, causing a massive short circuit. The Navy first used this missile during the opening minutes of Operation Desert Storm to knock out Saddam Hussein's air defenses and command facilities.

During Operation Desert Fox in December 1998, in which American warships and submarines conducted a 70-hour attack against Iraqi targets to reduce Saddam Hussein's ability to make weapons of mass destruction, the Navy launched more than 300 Tomahawk missiles. This depleted 10 percent of the Navy's inventory, and caused the service to anxiously rebuild its arsenal and speed the acquisition of an improved version of the long-range missile.

The Navy is now developing the Block IV Tomahawk Land-Attack Missile, which should be operational in 2003. Known as the Tactical Tomahawk, it will carry a warhead filled with smart submunitions (that is, bomblets that have sensing/homing capability). The missile can be

The Rolling Airframe Missile (RAM) launcher is quickly replacing the Phalanx CIWS as a warship's point defense weapon to "splash" incoming enemy aircraft and antiship missiles. RAM is an advanced, fire-and-forget missile that has a range of about 5 miles. *S. F. Tomajczyk*

reprogrammed while in flight to strike any of 15 preprogrammed alternate targets, or it can be sent new GPS coordinates to hit another target.

Amazingly, the Tactical Tomahawk will also be capable of loitering over a battlefield for several hours after dropping a portion of its submunitions. As it flies over the area, it will transmit images via its onboard TV camera to war-fighting commanders so they can assess damage done to the target. If necessary, they can then redirect the missile to any other target.

This high-tech weapon will be programmable from its launching warship or submarine. This is a tremendous step forward in naval combat. Why? Currently, a Tomahawk's flight path is downloaded from one of two cruise missile support activities in

Norfolk, Virginia, or Pearl Harbor, Hawaii. By allowing a destroyer, cruiser, or attack submarine to program its own Tomahawks, it will dramatically speed up the attack process and permit the vessel to accurately fire on mobile enemy targets and forces (such as SCUD missile launchers and troops) identified through the CVBG's intelligence efforts.

Spurred by the success of the Tomahawk, the Navy is also developing a kinetic-energy variant of the Tactical Tomahawk, which will be equipped with a special penetrator warhead to attack buried enemy command posts and bunkers. It will be capable of plowing through several layers of dirt, rock, concrete, and steel before detonating deep underground. The Navy has ordered 225 of these missiles.

Standard—The Standard missile is a series of surface-to-air and surface-to-surface missiles used by warships to protect themselves against enemy aircraft, ships, and low-altitude cruise missiles. Essentially, the Standard missile was produced in three major types: the SM-1 (MR), SM-2 (MR), and the SM-2 (ER). Since the SM-1 (MR) is only found aboard the Oliver Hazard Perry–class frigates, we'll focus on the SM-2 versions.

The SM-2 (MR) is a medium-range defensive weapon for Ticonderoga- and Arleigh Burke–class AEGIS warships. Launched from the vertical launch system, the SM-2 (MR) is a two-stage missile that features midcourse guidance and improved resistance to enemy jamming efforts. It has a range of about 40 to 90 miles and can hit targets flying at altitudes of 80,000 feet. It travels at speeds of Mach 2.5 and is equipped with semi-active radar homing and a high-explosive warhead that has a proximity fuse.

As for the SM-2 (ER), it is an extended-range surface-to-air missile that has an inertial guidance system with semi-active homing radar and a high-explosive warhead. It has a range of 65 to 100 miles.

The Navy is in the process of modifying up to 800 SM-2 missiles to the Land-Attack Standard Missile configuration. LASM will serve as an interim missile aboard AEGIS-equipped cruisers and destroyers until the Advanced Land-Attack Missile (ALAM) is eventually deployed on the Navy's futuristic DD-21 Land-Attack destroyer.

Vertical ASROC—The UUM-139 VL ASROC is a ship-to-submarine rocket that is launched from the vertical launch system. An indepth description of this weapon can be found in chapter 6.

Sinking Enemy Ships

While the vertical launch system has substantially strengthened the firepower of today's aircraft carrier battle group, it does pose a dilemma at times. For instance, when a guided-missile cruiser or destroyer heads for sea, the mix of missiles in its VLS is predetermined before it leaves the pier. Once the warship is deployed, it cannot change how many Tomahawks, Standards, or VL ASROCs it has in its cells. So if it runs low or runs out of a particular type of missile, the battle group commander must be made aware of this so he can make wise tactical decisions based on the remaining firepower. The last thing he would want to happen is to order a ship that is running low on antiship missiles to engage a heavily armed fleet of destroyers.

In addition to the VLS, modern surface combatants have other weapons systems available to them. One of the most important is the RGM-84 Harpoon, the Navy's principal antiship cruise missile. A subsonic, sea-skimming missile, the Harpoon is capable of striking enemy warships at distances of up to 166 miles. Target data is fed into the Harpoon before launching, including Over-The-Horizon radar sources, if available. Once launched, a radar altimeter maintains the missile's trajectory height.

As the Harpoon approaches its target, an active-radar terminal seeker searches and locks on to the enemy warship and commands the missile to abruptly pull up and swoop in on the vessel from above. This maneuver is designed to outsmart any point-defense weapons the warship may have, such as a gatling-style gun or antimissile rocket.

There are four variations of the Harpoon, the most notable being the RGM-84D. It enables the

On the bridge of a Ticonderoga-class guided-missile cruiser. One of the major changes in how warships operate on a day-to-day basis in today's Navy is the introduction of the Core/Flex program. The effort essentially reorganizes a ship's watch system to reduce fatigue and strain on the crew. Under the traditional system, as many as 10 watches were stood on the bridge, 18 in the CIC, and 13 in the engineering compartments. Under the new system, only 4 core watches are stood in the bridge, 7 in CIC, and 6 in engineering. When certain conditions arise, these core watch standers are joined by members of the Flex Watches. As for the circular-shaped devices located on the windows in this photo, they are designed to prevent fogging. It helps a warship to see where it is going, even if it does rely heavily on radar and technology to safely navigate the oceans of the world. *S. F. Tomajczyk*

missile to re-attack the target by flying a clover-leaf pattern if it fails to acquire the ship on the initial approach. It also has a larger fuel tank than the earlier models, nearly doubling its range from 88 miles to 166 miles.

A submarine-launched version of the Harpoon—designated UGM-84 Sub-Harpoon—is deployed aboard nuclear attack submarines. It is fitted with a shroud to permit it to fit a standard 21-inch torpedo tube for launching. When fired, a booster rocket drives the encapsulated missile up and out of the water where the capsule is jettisoned and the missile's turbojet engine ignites. Upon reaching an altitude of about 5,000 feet, the Sub-Harpoon then cruises at high subsonic speed (Mach 0.85) and low level to

Navigation done the old-fashioned way—with compass and ruler. This photo was taken aboard the amphibious assault ship USS *Nassau* (LHA-4) in the combat information center. *S. F. Tomajczyk*

thwart detection as it flies against enemy surface ships up to 105 nautical miles away.

Another noteworthy antiship missile is the AGM-119B Penguin. It is a supersonic (Mach 1.2), fire-and-forget missile that is launched from the Navy's SH-60B Seahawk LAMPS III antisubmarine helicopter, which is found aboard the Ticonderoga-, Spruance-, and Oliver Hazard Perry–class warships. Originally built for the Norwegian navy, the Penguin entered U.S. service in 1993. It has a range of about 22 miles and possesses an inertial guidance system, plus infrared terminal homing. It carries a 265-pound semi–armor piercing, high-explosive warhead on an indirect flight path from the helicopter to the unsuspecting enemy ship.

Defense! Defense!

To protect itself from surface attack while underway at sea, a CVBG establishes protective zones ("sectors") around it, which are aggressively patrolled by its destroyer and cruiser escorts. These warships use their arsenals to attack enemy ships, aircraft, and cruise missiles that are heading for the aircraft carrier. In situations like this, these same ships often find themselves in the crosshairs, usually with little more than just a handful of seconds to identify the threat and respond correctly. A ship's commanding officer

and his CIC have to make split-second decisions when they are suddenly confronted by a Sunburn cruise missile that is skimming along the wavetops at 1,736 miles per hour toward them.

Recognizing this danger, the Navy equips all its ships with self-defense weapons ("point defense"). The most common weapons are the Sea Sparrow, Rolling Airframe Missile, and the Phalanx Close-In Weapon System.

The RIM-7 Sea Sparrow is an offspring of the Sparrow radar-guided, air-to-air missile used by fighter aircraft. It is fired from a four-tube launcher that is generally located toward the stern of a surface combatant that does not have Standard missile capabilities. The solid-propellant missile may only weigh a mere 500 pounds and be 8 inches in diameter, but it travels at a lightning speed of 2,660 miles per hour and has a range of about 30 miles. The Sea Sparrow uses semi-active radar to home in on the hostile missile, and then destroys it with a 90-pound blast fragmentation warhead.

The U.S. Navy, along with a dozen NATO nations, is developing the Evolved Sea Sparrow Missile (ESSM), which has a range of 27 miles and can travel at speeds of Mach 3. The missile will be more responsive and capable of handling increased enemy antiship missile threats.

In the meantime, the Navy has been replacing its original Sea Sparrow system since 1991 with the U.S./German–designed Rolling Airframe Missile (RAM), an advanced, short-range, fire-and-forget missile used against air threats. The RAM missile, the only one in service with the Navy that rotates during flight, is 9 feet, 2 inches long, has a 5-inch diameter, and weighs 160 pounds. It uses existing technologies in its makeup: the infrared seeker from the Stinger missile and the solid-propellant rocket motor, fuse, and warhead (25 pounds of high explosive) from the Sidewinder missile. RAM, which has a range of 5.4 miles, can be fired from Sea Sparrow launchers and from its own uniquely designed 21-cell launcher. The missiles travel at Mach 2.

This angular and strange-looking ship is the *Sea Shadow*, a test craft built in the mid-1980s by Lockheed to secretly explore a variety of advanced technologies for warships, including ship control, structures, automation, sea-keeping, and signature control. Many of the technologies were incorporated into the design of the Arleigh Burke–class destroyers, as well as the Navy's ocean surveillance ships (T-AGOS). The 560-ton *Sea Shadow* was kept hidden inside a floating barge during the day to prevent people from seeing it; testing was done at night. In 1993, the Navy finally revealed the craft to the public, which enabled the Navy to conduct various tests during the day. The *Sea Shadow* was subsequently laid up in San Diego a year later. In March 1999, the craft was reactivated to support research and development efforts in designing the next generation destroyer, the DD-21 Land-Attack Destroyer. The 164-foot-long *Sea Shadow* is powered by a twin-screw, diesel-electric drive and has a crew of 10. She is supported above the water by two fin-like hulls that are attached to buoyant torpedo-like devices underwater. Such an arrangement offers increased sea-keeping capabilities, especially in heavy seas. *U.S. Navy*

The Phalanx Close-In Weapon System (CIWS, pronounced "See Whiz") is a 20-millimeter Gatling-style gun with six barrels that fire 4,500 rounds per minute. With a range of less than a mile, it is literally used as a ship's last-ditch effort to protect itself from aircraft and antiship missiles. The CIWS, which has a magazine capacity of 1,550 rounds, essentially creates a wall of armor-piercing, tungsten penetrators that the missile has to fly through to reach the ship. The system uses radar to track the inbound missile and a computer to determine where the gun must be pointed to strike the missile. The radar tracks both the missiles and the penetrators and corrects the gun's aim to bring the two together. If two or more missiles are approaching, CIWS automatically analyzes the threat and reacts to the most dangerous threat first.

Unfortunately, with advancements in foreign antiship missile technology, the Navy has decided to replace the Phalanx CIWS with the Rolling Airframe Missile. RAM is able to kill inbound cruise missiles at greater (and safer) distances from the Navy's warships.

There is yet another defensive measure surface combatants have to protect themselves from cruise missiles: chaff and decoys. In an *in extremis* situation, a warship can launch chaff (Mk-36 Rapid Bloom Off-Board Countermeasure) and active decoys to seduce the attention of an incoming missile and redirect its destination. The chaff, as mentioned in chapter 3, creates a huge radar return with its aluminized glass fibers for the missile to home in on, while the active decoys broadcast powerful signals to jam the missile's homing sensor. Infrared decoy flares can also be launched to lure heat-seeking missiles away from the ship.

Granted the missile may explode above, alongside, or just astern the ship and shower it with fragments, but the damage will be significantly less than if the ship had taken a direct hit. In naval surface warfare, it is better to have a close call than to visit Davy Jones' locker.

The USS *Seawolf* (SSN-21) at sea, the lead ship of the latest class of nuclear attack submarines. She and her two "sisters," the USS *Connecticut* and *Jimmy Carter,* will transition the Navy's so-called "Silent Service" to the next generation of Virginia-class (SSN-774) subs, which will begin entering service in 2004. The Seawolf submarines are faster, quieter, deeper diving, and stealthier than the aging Los Angeles–class subs. They also have twice as many torpedo tubes (including the introduction of a 30-inch-diameter tube) and 30 percent more weapons. *U.S. Navy*

Chapter 6

Antisubmarine Warfare
War Beneath the Waves

We must still have the capability to deal with the submarine threat. The submarine is a growth industry right now. There are lots of countries that have them and lots of countries that want them.

Admiral Jay Johnson, U.S. Navy Chief of Naval Operations

"To sink or significantly damage one of our aircraft carriers would be like winning the lottery for an adversary, striking an incredible blow to the world's predominant sea power," says Commander Bob Rawls, group staff tactical action officer aboard the nuclear-powered aircraft carrier USS *Carl Vinson* (CVN-70) in 1996, when the battle group was deployed to the Persian Gulf. "One of the cheapest and perhaps easiest ways to destroy an aircraft carrier is with a submarine. They represent stealth technology at its best, which is why battle groups have so many resources to hunt them down."

His concern about submarines is not uncommon. Sailors naturally turn a suspicious eye to the world's oceans, trying to see the menacing shadows of 350-foot-long steel eels slithering beneath the waves. Why? During World War II, a carrier battle group only had to worry about a submarine torpedo attack that could be launched within 4,000 yards. Today, with advancements in technology—most notably the deployment of submarine-launched antiship missiles—an enemy submarine can launch an attack against an aircraft carrier from more than 100 miles away. (The Soviet SS-N-19 has a range of 310 miles!) If the missile flies a depressed trajectory—literally skimming the wave crests at Mach 0.8 or faster—it can surprise a carrier battle group that is not on its toes, sending some 6,000 sailors to the bottom of the sea.

At this writing, there are more than 600 submarines being operated by 42 nations around the globe. So, as vast and empty as the ocean seemingly appears to the naked eye, it is deceptively crowded—and dangerous. An aircraft carrier is always in the crosshairs of enemy periscopes and in the dreams of submariners.

This is especially true since submarines routinely use Mother Nature's features to their own advantage. For instance, to avoid being detected by passing ships and aircraft, submarines often hide below the ocean's thermocline (a layer of dense, cold water that reflects and refracts sound waves) or deep scatter layer (a deep underwater zone made up of floating microscopic plants and animal life that scatter acoustic waves). With cunning, patience, and a little luck, a sub skipper can carefully position himself to fire a few "tin fish" at an aircraft carrier.

Complicating matters is the Navy's recent metamorphosis from a deep ocean, blue-water force to a shallow, brown-water force as a result of the break-up of the Soviet Union and, subsequently, the end of the Cold War. The Navy is now expected to operate its carriers, submarines, and surface ships in the fordable and confining waters close to foreign shores, such as the Persian Gulf. These littoral waters are infested with small, low-tech, diesel-electric submarines, which are extremely quiet. An enemy submarine captain, who knows the local currents and underwater features better than the Navy, can easily hide in the nooks and

The skipper's quarters aboard the USS *Miami* (SSN-755) may be small and mundane when compared to the large and well-decorated staterooms found aboard a surface warship, but it is cozy. Under the command of Commander Jim Ransom III, the USS *Miami* participated in the 70-hour assault against Iraq during Operation Desert Fox in December 1998. The sub launched an unspecified number of Tomahawk land-attack cruise missiles against Iraqi targets. The laptop computer that Commander Ransom is using allows him to exchange classified tactical information with the CVBG commander, as well as communicate with various Navy commands. *S. F. Tomajczyk*

crannies of the coastline, waiting for a target to pass and then launch an attack. A lumbering 97,000-ton aircraft carrier will have little time and confined maneuvering space to respond and defend itself.

To thwart submarine torpedo and missile attacks, a carrier battle group establishes a submarine exclusion zone around itself that extends outward for hundreds of miles. (The actual distance is classified and varies with the CVBG's operating area.) This zone is generally comprised of three perimeters: an outer, middle, and inner perimeter. Each zone has specific military resources, ranging from fixed-wing aircraft to helicopters and from sonobuoys and towed arrays to antisubmarine rockets.

This chapter takes an in-depth look at the little-publicized war fought beneath the waves. It is a war fought with technology and weapons, plus a lot of luck, persistence, and intuition.

The Outer Zone

To keep enemy submarines well beyond striking range of a carrier battle group, the Navy relies heavily on underwater sonar systems to detect their presence. The two most distinguished systems are the Surface Towed-Array Sonar System (SURTASS) and the Sound Surveillance System (SOSUS). Both serve as proverbial "trip wires," alerting the National Command Authority that an intruder has trespassed and is operating in a particular region of the ocean. Subsequently, long-range surveillance aircraft, such as the antisubmarine warfare turboprop P-3C Orion, are sent out to investigate the situation by sowing the ocean with sonobuoys to monitor the submarine's whereabouts. In wartime, the P-3C would drop high-speed homing torpedoes and depth charges to destroy the hostile submarine long before it poses a threat to the carrier battle group.

SURTASS is a passive sonar array that is towed behind the Navy's Stalwart-class and Victorious-class ocean surveillance ships. It is made up of a hydrophone array at the end of a 6,000-foot-long neutrally buoyant cable, which is towed at the turtle-pace speed of 3 knots so the system can compile underwater sounds made by enemy submarines. The signals are analyzed by the ship's computers before they are relayed in real-time to one of two naval shore-based processing centers—one on each coast of the United States—via a super high-frequency SATCOM link. Once the target data is processed, it is sent out to long-range surveillance aircraft and naval vessels at sea so they can hunt down the submarine. Because the SURTASS array resembles a long strand of spaghetti, it is nicknamed "the noodle" by Navy personnel.

SOSUS is an underwater network of passive sonar detectors and hydrophones anchored on the ocean floor to detect noises made by passing submarines.

Such arrays are usually located near natural choke points around the globe where enemy shipping is forced to pass through. The individual sensor stations that make up a SOSUS array are carefully positioned in clusters 5 to 15 miles apart and are connected by fiber-optical cables to shore stations, which either process the data or send it via the Navy's UHF/SHF fleet satellite communications system (FLTSAT-COM) to a data-processing facility. SOSUS is so sensitive that it can detect engine noise at a distance of several hundred miles and locate its position to within a 9-mile radius.

SOSUS is also used to record identifying sound characteristics (or "signatures") that uniquely distinguish one ship or submarine from another. This information is stored on computer, allowing U.S. naval forces to immediately identify any noise their passive sonar systems pick up and determine from what ship—by name, class, and nationality—it came from. This was demonstrated in the movie, *The Hunt for Red October.*

The first SOSUS network, codenamed Caesar, was laid on the ocean floor off of Sandy Hook, New York, followed by hydrophone installations off Eleuthera in the Bahamas. The Navy publicly acknowledges the existence of only six SOSUS networks: across the gap between Greenland, Iceland, and the United Kingdom (also known as the GIUK Gap); the Bering Strait (between the Aleutian Islands and Japan); the Strait of Gibraltar (between North Africa and Portugal); the gap between Norway and Svalbard in the Norwegian Sea; across the Denmark Strait; and along the West Coast of the United States (codenamed "Colossus"). Other SOSUS arrays are believed to be located as follows: the Gulf Coast of the United States; between Taiwan and the Philippines; between Italy and Corsica; off the coast of Turkey near the Black Sea; off the coast of Diego Garcia in the Indian Ocean; near Hawaii; parallel to the Kuril Islands north of Japan; off the Aleutians; and across the Davis Strait between Canada and Greenland. Two additional sites are suspected to be located off the

Up periscope! You can do just about anything with an attack sub's periscope, except fly to the moon. The sophisticated equipment has a variety of magnification modes, plus infrared and high-contrast viewing capabilities. When an officer looks through the periscope, it's referred to as "Dancing with the One-Eyed Lady." You can tell how much use a periscope gets by examining the periscope about waist high, where the metal belt buckles worn by the officers rub against it. In this photo, the brassing is evident below the lieutenant's right biceps. *S. F. Tomajczyk*

coast of Northwest Cape in Australia and Christmas Island in the Indian Ocean.

Although SOSUS is expected to be an early target for jamming, deception, and outright destruction in wartime by enemy forces, it will serve a valuable role

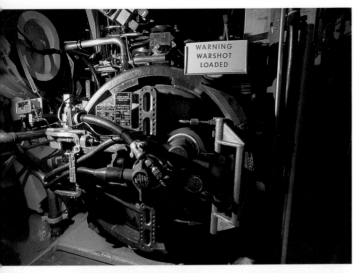

One of four 21-inch-diameter torpedo tubes found aboard the USS *Miami*. Attack subs rely on the Mk-48 ADCAP (advanced capability) torpedo to sink enemy submarines and warships. The 19-foot-long torpedo, which weighs 3,450 pounds, can speed along at 55 knots for up to 20 miles. As it slices through the water, a thin guidance wire unwinds behind it, allowing the fire control operator aboard the submarine to receive acoustic information and then fine-tune the torpedo's course. The Mk-48 has both passive and active homing, and its warhead contains approximately 650 pounds of high explosive. *S. F. Tomajczyk*

in tracking the immediate prewar movements of enemy shipping.

For instance, if a hostile submarine is detected by the Strait of Gibraltar SOSUS array heading out toward an aircraft carrier battle group steaming off the Atlantic coast of North Africa, P-3C Orion long-range surveillance aircraft can be scrambled from Lajes Field on Terceira Island in the Azores to track it down. The Orion, which has a range of 2,750 miles and a mission endurance of 14 hours, seeds the ocean near the sub with passive and active sonobuoys and uses a magnetic anomaly detector (MAD, a quasi-metal detector that extends from the tail like a bee stinger) to pinpoint the sub's location. In

wartime, this data is used by the aircrew to determine when and where to drop a deep-diving, high-speed Mk-46 torpedo or a Mk-101 depth charge on the sub from the plane's internal weapons bay or underwing pylons. The P-3C Orion can carry 20,000 pounds worth of bombs, torpedoes, missiles, and mines, including the B-57 nuclear depth charge, which has a yield of 5 to 10 kilotons.

Although the Navy began shutting down a portion of its aging $16 billion SOSUS system in 1994 to cut costs, it does not mean that the United States has gone "deaf" underwater. Quite the contrary, SOSUS is being supplemented—and will eventually be replaced—with a new, highly classified underwater sonar surveillance program known as the Fixed Distribution System (FDS). Like SOSUS, FDS will listen for submarines at specific locations or choke points around the world. When a target is heard, P-3 Orions and naval vessels will be sent in to investigate and, if necessary, destroy the submarine.

The Middle Zone

The best and ultimate weapon to use against a submarine is another submarine. That is because they both operate in the same environment, they both use similar attack and defensive tactics, they both can perform below the thermocline and deep scatter layer, and they are outfitted with nearly identical, deadly weapons. This fact is not lost on the U.S. Navy: It assigns two nuclear-attack submarines (SSN) to escort every carrier battle group. These so-called "hunter/killer" subs usually prowl the ocean some 100 to 300 miles ahead of the aircraft carrier, using their sophisticated sensors to silently detect, hunt down, and destroy enemy submarines. The reason they are positioned so far ahead of the battle group is that the racket made by the cavitating propellers from the destroyers, cruisers, frigates, and so on would interfere with the SSN's ability to hear enemy subs if they were any closer. An aircraft carrier battle group can easily be heard up to 100 miles away by sonar.

The major drawback to using SSNs is that their sensing ability outstrips the performance of their weapons. In other words, their passive sonar systems can detect a hostile sub at distances much greater than their torpedoes can travel. This means an SSN must continue to close in to a target after detecting its presence (at the risk of possibly being discovered itself) just to get off a shot.

Today, there are two major classes of attack submarines in operation with the Navy: the Los Angeles–class (SSN 688) and the Seawolf-class (SSN 21).

There are 53 Los Angeles–class submarines currently in service with the Navy. Measuring the length of a football field from goal post to goal post, the 688-class is one of the most sophisticated and deadly hunter/killers ever to stalk the world's oceans, with an operational depth of 980 feet. (Its maximum diving depth is alleged to be 1,400 feet.) At the heart of its ability to detect hostile subs is the digital BQQ-5 sonar system, which uses both hull-mounted and towed acoustic hydrophone arrays. Each submarine has six large, rectangular-shaped hydrophone "patches" (called "wide aperture array") affixed to its hull, three on the port and three on the starboard. The passive wide aperture arrays are positioned near the bow, midship, and on the stern to pick out man-made noises from the clamor made by sea life.

As for the towed acoustical arrays, there are two types in use by Los Angeles–class subs today: the TB-16 and TB-23. The TB-16 is a so-called "thick line" system that is normally stowed in a tube running outside the submarine's pressure hull, with the winch, cable, and reel located in the forward main ballast tank. When the submarine is submerged at sea, it unwinds the 3-inch-thick, 225-foot-long acoustic module so that it trails nearly 1/2 mile behind it at the end of a 1/2-inch-diameter cable. The module is tapered at both ends to minimize any flow noise that might interfere with the sensor's performance.

The TB-23 (thin line array) is a more advanced and lightweight version of the TB-16, which it is

A Tomahawk land-attack cruise missile clears the ocean and leaps into the air after being launched from a VLS tube aboard the USS *Pittsburgh* (SSN-720) during Operation Desert Storm in 1991. Nuclear attack submarines are being used more often for missions like this since they can approach an enemy target more closely and quietly than a surface warship. After launching a salvo of missiles, they simply disappear into the murky depths of the ocean. This photo was taken through the USS *Pittsburgh's* periscope. *U.S. Navy*

replacing as submarine sonar systems are upgraded. Instead of being stored in a tube on the pressure hull, the TB-23 is reeled directly into the submarine's main ballast tank.

Using its towed array, a 688-class submarine can quietly listen for sounds made by enemy submarines

In the sonar room of a Los Angeles–class nuclear attack submarine, three sonarmen classify their contacts by listening to them over headsets and monitoring their sound signatures, which cascade like a waterfall on a video screen in front of them. The entire room is dimmed, which enhances the cathode-ray tube displays.

"Subs aren't as quiet as you think," says a sonarman aboard the USS *Miami* (SSN-755), pressing a hand to his right earphone. "Every vessel has a peculiarity that gives it a special sound, a unique piece of gear, a different propeller, an unusual engine. The clue that gives a submarine away is the swishing sound of suppressed cavitation. That's what I listen for."

A submarine not silent? For decades now, the submarine forces of the world have been referred to as the Silent Service for two reasons. First, submariners are unable to discuss their classified missions with anyone, necessitating a so-called "buttoned-lip" mentality. And second, noise is the natural enemy of a submarine, which relies on silence and stealth to make a successful attack.

Yet the sonarman was quite correct: Submarines are not silent and they certainly are not undetectable. The U.S. Navy relies on a number of scientific facts about a submarine to locate it in the depths of the world's ocean.

• Hydrodynamic noise—A submerged submarine creates hydrodynamic noise, which results from water flowing over the hull. It is intensified by protrusions and orifices, such as antenna masts and free-flood holes. Another source of hydrodynamic noise is a sub's towed array. If the sub travels too fast, the cable may begin to vibrate at its natural frequency.

• Propeller noise—When a sub's propellers rotate, air bubbles at the blade tips collapse with a hiss, radiating mostly in a horizontal plane in line with the blades. This hissing sound increases with the momentum of the sub's propellers and is most conspicuous during acceleration and fast maneuvers.

• Mechanical noise—A submarine is filled with operating machinery and rotating parts, including turbine blades, gear trains, and pumps. Nuclear subs are even noisier than diesel-electric submarines, with closed-loop cooling systems to keep the reactor within safe operating limits.

• Magnetic effects—The large metal hull of a submarine is constantly cutting through and disrupting the lines of the Earth's magnetic field. This creates a so-called "magnetic anomaly" that is detectable by airborne sensors. Additionally, subs generate their own electrical and magnetic fields, which are created through an electro-chemical process as water flows over the hull.

• Wake—Like all ships, a submarine leaves a wake as it travels underwater. This wake can be detected by active sonar. Furthermore, the turbulence eventually reaches the ocean's surface, where it disrupts the wave pattern. This variation is detectable by the Navy's Over-the-Horizon Backscatter (OTH-B) radar system.

• Thermal differences—The wake turbulence created by a submarine sometimes causes cold water to rise and mix with warmer surface water. This temperature difference is easily sensed by infrared sensors placed aboard satellites and aircraft.

• Wave height—When a submarine moves through shallow water, it causes a small, perceptible rise in the surface of the water above the hull. This slight increase in wave height is potentially detectable by satellites that are equipped with a radio altimeter.

• Exhaust—Although nuclear-powered submarines do not have to come to the surface to obtain air to run their engines and recharge their batteries, diesel-electric powered submarines (SSK) do this daily. Exhaust fumes from the submarine's snorkel tube are detectable from miles away by "sniffers" mounted on ASW aircraft.

(such as hydrodynamic noise, machinery sound, and propeller cavitation) operating at great distances. More important, though, it can hear submarines directly behind it—in the baffles—where, traditionally, a sub is deaf due to the noise made by its own propellers.

All noise detected by the towed array is processed by the submarine's BSY-1 integrated sonar and fire-control system, which also collects and analyzes sounds detected by the wide aperture array and the submarine's powerful low-frequency sonar, SADS. (Note: The spherical-shaped, passive/active sonar is enormous, filling the entire bow of the submarine.) The BSY-1 scrutinizes, classifies, and tracks the noise, constantly calculating and recalculating torpedo (or missile) firing solutions. These launch instructions are fed directly to the weapons by the BSY-1, allowing the sub's skipper to fire quickly and accurately.

Since the submarine's BQQ-5 sonar system is able to detect hostile targets farther away than its torpedoes can travel, the captain must either move in closer or resort to launching a missile. Neither option is safe: To fire a missile is to give away your precise location, inviting immediate (and violent!) retaliation, while to close in with the target means to risk being detected by its sonar system. Fortunately, Los Angeles nuclear attack submarines were designed with these specific hazards in mind.

First, their hulls are coated with anechoic tiles, a special rubberized substance that absorbs sonar waves. This helps prevent an enemy sub from getting a fix on the 688's location using active sonar, much less an indication of its presence in the ocean.

Second, the overall shape of the submarine and its external features are designed to minimize noise production; water flows smoothly and quietly around the ship as it travels underwater.

Third, the sub's inner compartments are free floating, which means internal noise (such as machinery, conversation, and closing hatches) is not easily transmitted through the hull.

The USS *Annapolis* (SSN-760) shown pierside at the submarine base in New London, Connecticut. Security is extremely high since classified ASW technologies are constantly being added to submarines. This photo shows several interesting things, including the 12-tube vertical launch system located in the bow from which Tomahawk missiles are fired; the blister-tube running the starboard length of the sub that houses the TB-16 "thick line" towed acoustical array; and the rubberized anechoic tiles that blanket the sub's hull to prevent enemy sonar detection. *S. F. Tomajczyk*

Fourth, before being sent out on patrol, each submarine's magnetic field is significantly reduced through a process known as degaussing. This helps the submarine avoid being detected by airborne and towed MAD sensors.

Fifth, a variety of expendable countermeasures are available to each submarine to thwart an enemy torpedo attack. The decoys (ADC Mk2s) are ejected from the submarine and either jam the incoming torpedo's homing sensor or attract it with an acoustical signal while the submarine leaves the area.

And last, the submarine's pressurized-water reactor, which produces 30,000 horsepower, enables it to sprint at speeds in excess of 35 knots when submerged to quickly intercept a target, fire either a missile or torpedo, and then escape.

Driving a submarine without having any windows to look out of is disconcerting; you have to rely on the accuracy of your instruments. Here, a chief oversees the steering of the USS *Miami* by three helmsmen. In the same small room, known as the control center ("conn"), are the two periscopes, the navigation center, and the weapons fire-control center. It makes for a very busy and cramped environment. *S. F. Tomajczyk*

The Los Angeles–class submarines bristle with weapons. For combat purposes, they have four 21-inch torpedo tubes amidship, through which the Mk-48 Advanced Capability torpedo is fired. This torpedo is 19 feet, 2 inches long and weighs 3,450 pounds. Twin, contra-rotating propellers drive the torpedo along at a blinding speed of 55 knots. Its range, although classified, is estimated to be about 20 miles; its diving depth is about 3,000 feet.

When launched, the torpedo unwinds a thin guidance wire through which it sends acoustic information back to the submarine as well as receives instructions from the fire control center. This enables an operator in the submarine to initially guide the torpedo toward the target while avoiding decoys and jamming devices that might be deployed by the enemy sub. The Mk-48 can use either active or passive acoustic homing to intercept the hostile target. If it somehow misses, it is programmed to automatically re-attack several times. The warhead contains approximately 650 pounds of high explosive, more than adequate to sink an enemy submarine. The torpedo detonates below the sub, buckling and rupturing its hull with the blast wave.

Although the Los Angeles–class submarines could be classified by Hollywood as a "Lethal Weapon," the Navy's newest class of nuclear attack submarine, the Seawolf-class, is definitely a "Rambo." The 353-foot-long multimission submarines are not only faster, quieter, deeper diving, and stealthier, but they have twice as many torpedo tubes and carry 30 percent more weapons. They also introduce the 30-inch-diameter launch tube to American submarines, which will enable them to fire larger weapons in the future. The class is intended to bridge the evolution from the aging Los Angeles–class submarines to the sophisticated Virginia-class (SSN-774) attack subs, the first of which will be launched in 2004.

The $2.5 billion lead ship, the USS *Seawolf* (SSN-21), was commissioned in July 1997. At the heart of the *Seawolf* is the BSY-2 advanced combat system. It combines data from the sub's active sonar, wide aperture array, passive towed array sonar (the TB-23 *and* TB-16), a Mine and Ice Detection Avoidance Sonar (MIDAS), and the combat control system with an advanced computer system, which is designed to detect, classify, track, and launch weapons at enemy targets. The development of the BSY-2 is considered to be the largest computer software effort ever undertaken for a submarine.

The *Seawolf* is able to carry out multiple missions, including surveillance, intelligence collection, special warfare, covert cruise missile strike, mine warfare, and antisubmarine and antisurface warfare.

At this writing, two of the three Seawolf submarines have been commissioned, the *Seawolf* (SSN 21) and the *Connecticut* (SSN 22). The third submarine, named in honor of the only president to serve aboard a sub, Jimmy Carter, is under construction at Groton, Connecticut, and is scheduled to be delivered to the Navy in 2002. The reason only three subs are being built, and not the 30 or so originally envisioned, is that the ship was designed to fight the Soviet submarine threat of the 21st century, a danger that no longer exists. Today, the underwater threat lies in the shallow littoral regions of the world where some 100 ultraquiet diesel-electric subs reign; the forthcoming Virginia-class submarines are designed to address this emerging peril.

Backing up the battle group's nuclear attack submarines in the hunt for hostile subs is the S-3B Viking antisubmarine (ASW) aircraft. It stands ever vigilant to swoop in and give a sub skipper a run for his money. With a range of 2,300 miles and a mission endurance of seven to nine hours, the Viking typically operates in the middle and outer carrier battle group ASW zones, searching for threats. It is an extremely sophisticated aircraft equipped with advanced detection and data display/processing capabilities, which provide a real-time link between the four-man crew and the various surface and underwater sensors.

The $27 million Viking has a high-resolution radar for maritime reconnaissance that is able to detect submarine periscopes that are briefly exposed, even in rough seas. It is also equipped with forward-looking infrared (FLIR), a retractable MAD boom, an inverse synthetic aperture radar (ISAR) imaging system to allow for ship classification at long range, a passive electronic countermeasures receiving and frequency measuring system, and 60 active/passive sonobuoys for submarine detection.

When hunting for a sub, the Viking deploys its sonobuoys in a pattern over a wide area of ocean where the submarine is believed to be hiding. The sonobuoys are dropped from tubes located in the aft underbelly section of the plane. When they strike the ocean, the seawater-activated battery system is energized. A floating antenna is raised while the rest of the buoy sinks to a predetermined depth and begins to collect acoustical data, which is then transmitted to the aircraft. Depending on the model, the sonobuoys operate for as long as eight hours, constantly providing target-bearing information that is subsequently processed by the Viking's onboard computer.

When the sub's general location is determined, as evident by the acoustical data, its precise position is pinpointed by the plane's MAD boom. The sensor operator (SENSO) and tactical coordinator (TACCO) work closely together to locate the hiding sub and then determine the best way to attack it.

The S-3B Viking is generally armed with four Mk-46 Lightweight or Mk-50 Barracuda homing torpedoes (or a similar number of depth charges, bombs, or mines) in the weapons bay. The Mk-46 Lightweight torpedo, which is the NATO standard for antisubmarine warfare, is a deep-diving, high-speed torpedo equipped with active/passive acoustic homing. After it hits the water, it begins a helical search pattern until it detects the enemy submarine. It then attacks at a speed of about 45 knots. If it misses, it automatically reacquires the sub and continues with the attack. The torpedo has a range of about 7 miles and can dive to more than 1,200 feet. Its warhead consists of 95 pounds of PBXN-103 high explosive.

The Mk-50 Advanced Lightweight torpedo, the Barracuda, is the latest addition to the Navy's arsenal. It is similar to the Mk-46, but it's faster, has greater endurance, and can dive deeper. It also has better terminal homing, a programmable digital computer, and more destructive power. The 750-pound Barracuda is powered by a unique, stored chemical-energy propulsion system, which provides full power at all depths and can furnish multispeed settings as required by the situation at hand. The Mk-50 reportedly has a speed in excess of 50 knots and a maximum diving depth of about 1,950 feet. It has a 100-pound high-explosive, shaped charge. For maximum damage, the directed energy must penetrate the enemy sub's hull and not glance off.

In addition to the torpedoes, the S-3B Viking can also carry weapons on two underwing pylons, including rocket pods, cluster bombs, AGM-65F Maverick infrared-guided missiles, or AGM-84 Harpoon antiship missiles.

Because of the S-3B Viking's vital and deadly role in antisubmarine warfare, each aircraft carrier has a squadron of six to eight aircraft assigned to its air wing.

The Inner Zone

The area immediately surrounding an aircraft carrier battle group is referred to as the torpedo danger zone (TDZ). The radius of the zone is essentially the range at which a torpedo could successfully be fired by a hostile submarine and hit the ships. This circle, whose radius is also influenced by the battle group commander's assessment of the capabilities and tactics of the enemy's submarine force, advances with the main body of the battle group and grows in size with its cruise speed.

The torpedo danger zone is actively patrolled by ASW helicopters and a screen of ASW frigates and destroyers to discourage an attack. Each is assigned a specific sector of ocean (normally 65 to 80 square miles) to search and defend. The frigates and destroyers maneuver constantly to deny attacking subs the information they need to set up a firing solution for their torpedoes and antiship missiles. Likewise, the main body of the battle group follows a zigzagging course, which restricts its speed of advance to about 10 knots or so.

The larger, slow-moving surface ships, which make tempting targets, often tow decoys behind them to confuse incoming torpedoes. Known collectively as "nixies," these decoys emit either simulated propeller or machinery noises to lure passive-homing torpedoes away from the real ship, or powerful signals to jam an acoustic-homing torpedo's sensors, thereby denying it from acquiring the ship. The SLQ-25 nixie does both. A ship streams two of these small, lightweight countermeasures at a time in case one is hit by a decoyed torpedo. This practice ensures that a ship is not defenseless against a salvo torpedo attack.

Currently, the U.S. Navy and Royal Navy are jointly developing a new antitorpedo defense system, the Surface Ship Torpedo Defense (SSTD), to protect their warships against attack from any projected torpedo technologies. The classified project's top priority is to counter wake-homing torpedoes, which lock on to the turbulence created by a passing ship and have a 40-plus-mile range.

Unlike the V-3 Viking, P-3 Orion, and nuclear attack submarines that rely mainly on passive sonar to detect the presence of enemy submarines in the two outer ASW zones, the helicopters and surface ships in the torpedo danger zone often use active sonar to keep subs at arm's length from the battle group. The primary reason for this tactic is time constraints: It takes a high-speed torpedo only about 200 seconds to travel 5,000 yards. That means a carrier battle group has a little more than three minutes to detect a torpedo and take appropriate defensive actions before being struck. For small, fast-moving frigates, that poses no problem. But for lumbering aircraft carriers and replenishment ships, it is a near-impossible effort. Thus, to gain more reaction time, the battle group uses active sonar to "push" enemy subs farther away from itself, using the threat of detection and attack to its advantage.

Whenever a nearby submarine contact is made by any ship or aircraft in the carrier battle group, the main body turns away from the estimated position of the sub while several ASW units are released from their sectors by the CVBG commander to proceed at full speed toward the submarine's estimated position. Arriving on station, they then use active sonar to locate the submarine and launch an attack against it. Throughout this effort, data from the aircraft and warships is constantly shared with the battle group through the Anti-Submarine Classification and Analysis Center (ASCAC), which is installed aboard Nimitz-class aircraft carriers. ASCAC permits real-time sharing of data between the carrier, its ASW aircraft, and task force escorts.

Typically a carrier battle group's response to a submarine threat is predetermined. Various scenarios are anticipated and specific actions are drawn up before the battle group heads out to sea. The ships, for instance, will respond much differently to a submarine threat located 5 miles astern and moving at 12 knots than to an enemy sub positioned 2 miles dead ahead and closing at 20 knots. Creating these response plans ahead of time allows the ships that comprise the carrier battle group to collectively alter their course immediately and smoothly, without further communication from the CVBG commander when a threat suddenly appears.

Torpedoes launched by an enemy submarine are easily detected by warships due to the high-pitch whine produced by the fast-moving weapon's propellers. While modern acoustic-homing torpedoes can, admittedly, be difficult to evade, certain countermeasures can be taken. For instance, a ship can aggressively maneuver itself to present as narrow a profile as possible by pointing its bow at the torpedo. If there is not enough time to do this, however, the ship can alter its course 90 degrees across the torpedo's track and launch nixie noisemakers.

Although many of the 10 to 12 ships in an aircraft carrier battle group possess some capability to fight submarines, the primary antisubmarine warfare role rests squarely with the Oliver Hazard Perry–class of guided-missile frigates (FFG-7) and Spruance-class destroyers (DD-963). They are backed-up by the Ticonderoga-class guided missile cruisers and Arleigh Burke–class guided-missile destroyers, both of which are multimission surface combatants.

The Perry-class is a robust platform, armed with six Mk-46 torpedoes, Harpoon antiship missiles, Standard-MR SM-1 surface-to-air missiles, a 76-millimeter rapid-fire gun, and a Phalanx close-in weapons system "gatling" gun. Its most useful ASW weapons are the two SH-60B LAMPS III Seahawk helicopters deployed on most ships in this class. (Note: The aging and less capable SH-2 LAMPS I Seasprite, which entered service in 1973, is found

The sonar room aboard the USS *Miami*. These sonarmen and the sub's sensitive acoustic sensors spend their days listening to the noisy ocean around them, ever alert to the faint but distinct noise made by enemy ships and submarines. Using towed acoustic arrays and hull-mounted wide-aperture arrays, an attack submarine can easily detect targets hundreds of miles away. The sub's integrated sonar and fire-control system scrutinizes, classifies, and tracks any noise, constantly calculating torpedo or missile firing solutions. *S. F. Tomajczyk*

aboard some frigates.) That's because the Seahawk, which has a mission endurance of 3.5 hours and is equipped with sonobuoys, a dipping sonar, and three Mk-46 Lightweight or Mk-50 Barracuda torpedoes, extends the frigate's "eyes" and tactical combat power well over the horizon. This allows the frigate to successfully attack enemy submarines before they pose a deadly threat to the aircraft carrier battle group.

The LAMPS III Seahawk is deployed from the fantail of the frigate when a submarine is detected by the warship's SQS-56 hull-mounted sonar or SQR-19 TACTASS towed passive sonar array. (The latter is towed at variable depths up to 1,000 feet below the ocean's surface.) The helicopter flies out to the target area and drops sonobuoys into the water in a pattern that will entrap the submarine. The sonobuoys are

An extremely rare photo showing the USS *Scranton* (SSN-756) surfacing next to the USS *George Washington* (CVN-73) in the North Arabian Sea. The nuclear attack submarine has assumed a greater role in CVBG operations in recent years. Battle group commanders now value them to perform a variety of missions instead of their previous ASW role, including reconnaissance, SIGINT, covert insertion/extraction of special forces, and conducting strikes against land-based targets with the Tomahawk (TLAM) missile. *U.S. Navy*

deployed from a 25-tube pneumatic launcher located on the port side of the aircraft fuselage behind the cabin door. Sounds detected by the sonobuoys are transmitted by radio frequency to the Seahawk where they are analyzed and then forwarded to the frigate for further interpretation by computer and analysis by personnel in the combat information center (that means the air tactical control officer, acoustic sensor operator, remote radar operator, or ESM operator). When the submarine's location has been narrowed down, the helicopter descends to confirm its position

by either lowering an active sonar into the ocean (this is called "dipping sonar") or trailing a retractable MAD sensor (called a "bird") behind the aircraft. A high-speed, deep-diving torpedo is launched when the submarine is finally pinpointed.

The Seahawks use the AQS-13F or AQS-18 passive/active dipping sonar. Both systems have a range up to 11 miles and can operate in depths in excess of 1,000 feet from a 50-foot hover. The sonar are designed to detect and maintain contact with the submarine, while accurately determining its range and bearing. The Navy's newest is the low-frequency dipping sonar, the Airborne Low Frequency Sonar (ALPS), which is replacing the AQS-13F. Additionally, the Navy is developing the High Performance Active Sonar System (HIPAS), an active/passive dipping sonar that is intended to detect and track the most technologically advanced submarines.

The SH-60B Seahawk is equipped with RAST (Recovery Assist, Secure, and Traverse), a cable-and-winch system that quickly pulls a hovering helicopter downward to the ship's landing pad. This enables the helicopter to land on the pitching deck of a frigate, cruiser, or destroyer in extremely rough sea conditions, even when the ship is rolling through 28 degrees. Hence, the Seahawk can perform its vital ASW role in nearly any type of weather, except hurricanes, of course.

In addition to being deployed on the Oliver Hazard Perry–class frigates, the LAMPS III Seahawk is also found aboard many destroyers and guided-missile cruisers.

The sleek and uncluttered-looking Spruance-class destroyers (DD-963), which were commissioned between 1975 and 1983, were originally constructed as specialized ASW warships. They were eventually equipped for the antiship and land-attack roles with the addition of the Tomahawk cruise missile. Focusing on the Spruance's ASW mission here, though, the destroyers are outfitted with an impressive array of sensors, including the SQS-53C bow sonar—the Battle Group Sonar—that can operate in a variety of active and passive modes (such as surface duct, bottom bounce, and convergence zone). The system is so powerful and effective that the Navy decided not to install the hull-mounted variable depth sensor, a weighted, towed sonar array that can be "sunk" to various depths up to 600 feet.

As for ASW weapons, the destroyers have two three-tube torpedo launchers hidden behind sliding doors on either side of the superstructure. Each ship carries 14 Mk-46 torpedoes. Additionally, the destroyers carry two SH-60B LAMPS III Seahawk helicopters to hunt down and destroy enemy submarines over the horizon.

And last, 24 of the 27 Spruance-class destroyers have been upgraded to have the Mk-41 Vertical Launch System, which has a magazine capacity of 61 Tomahawk cruise missiles. The Vertical Launched ASROC (VLA), also found aboard Ticonderoga-class cruisers and Arleigh Burke–class guided-missile destroyers, consists of a Mk-46 Lightweight homing torpedo strapped to a solid-propellant rocket motor. After the 16-foot-long missile is launched at an enemy submarine, the booster is jettisoned at a predetermined point and the payload continues to follow a ballistic flight until a parachute deploys to gently lower the torpedo and its protective casing to the ocean. Upon entering the water, the protective nose cap breaks apart and the parachute cuts free. The torpedo's motor starts and its homing sensors become active. It goes into a search mode to locate and then attack the enemy submarine. Although classified, the VLA reportedly has a range of 16 miles.

The Navy also has a nuclear version of ASROC in its inventory. It has a 1-kiloton nuclear depth charge that is violent enough to sink any submarine within a 3-mile radius. Unlike the conventional VLA, which uses a parachute to slow its descent, the nuclear warhead free falls into the ocean and then detonates at a set depth. The nuclear ASROC was withdrawn by the Navy from active service in 1989, but it remains in the arsenal for possible future use. After all, no one knows who America's enemies will be in the years and decades ahead, or what weapons they will employ against us. However, it is a certainty that the lethal and stealthy submarine will be one of the tools slithering through the deep oceans in search of our aircraft carriers.

Fortunately, the U.S. Navy is vigilant and prepared for that eventuality. Using high-tech sensors and weapons, the aircraft carrier battle group is always willing to hunt down and send a rogue sub to the bottom of the ocean.

An LCAC ("Hopper") rushes up onto Onslow Beach at Camp Lejeune in North Carolina at 15 knots carrying a payload weighing up to 70 tons. Amphibious assault training exercises, such as this one, mimic real-world combat conditions as much as possible, heeding the advice: Train as you fight. *S. F. Tomajczyk*

Chapter 7

Amphibious Assault
Hitting the Beaches

It is 0430 hours and the aircraft hangar of the amphibious assault ship USS *Bataan* (LHD-5) is filled with hundreds of heavily armed Marines busily checking their 5.56-millimeter M-16A2 rifles and painting their faces in shades of green. They are preparing for combat, and the air is filled with tension. In the level immediately below them, the flooded well dock is drowning in the high-pitched noise of three idling hovercraft, known as LCACs for Landing Craft, Air Cushion, that will transport the Marines and their equipment to enemy beaches located over the horizon.

Meanwhile, on the *Bataan's* dark flight deck, the CH-46E Sea Knight and CH-53E Super Stallion helicopters are revving up, their cargo space filled with a Marine attack element. Their mission is to take over an enemy-held airport several miles inland from the beach. They will be protected from the air by AV-8B Harrier "jump jets" and AH-1W Super Cobra attack helicopters, which are also in the last stages of preparation to fly off the Bataan.

The *Bataan* is not the only ship that is busy at this early morning hour. Close by, aboard the USS *Whidbey Island* (LSD-41) and USS *Shreveport* (LPD-12), Marines are busy loading their LAV-25s, Humvees, 155-millimeter howitzers, and personal gear aboard LCACs and other landing craft.

> *Forward deployed forces, primarily naval expeditionary forces—the Navy-Marine Corps team—are vital to regional stability and to keeping crises from escalation into full-scale wars. To those who argue that the United States cannot afford to have this degree of vigilance anymore, we say: The United States can't afford not to.*
>
> Admiral Jay Johnson, Chief of Naval Operations, and General Charles C. Krulak, Commandant of the Marine Corps

If all goes well, the airport will be taken and the first wave of Marines will land on the beach *before* the sun rises, just an hour-and-a-half from now.

Welcome to the intense and noisy world of amphibious warfare.

From the Sea: the U.S. Marines

With 80 percent of the world's population living within 200 miles of the ocean, it makes sense that America's military forces have to be well-equipped and adept at conducting amphibious operations. At the heart of this force is the amphibious ready group (ARG), which is comprised of three or four amphibious ships and 2,200 combat-ready Marines of a marine expeditionary unit (MEU).

The U.S. Marine Corps, which is expressly charged with projecting sea power ashore, maintains two fleet Marine forces that total some 90,000 Marines. One is assigned to the Atlantic (Camp Lejeune, North Carolina) and the other to the Pacific (Camp H. M. Smith, Hawaii). Each fleet Marine force is organized into Marine air-ground task forces (MAGTFs), the size of which fluctuates with the mission and the size and strength of the enemy.

For instance, an MEU, considered to be the basic building block of all MAGTFs, is made up of about 2,000 Marines commanded by a colonel. Able to be

Marines of the 22d MEU (SOC) rush ashore before dawn in the first wave of an amphibious assault that took place during the USS *Kennedy* battle group's joint task force exercise (JTFEX) in July 1999. This beach is supposedly located in the fictitious nation, Kartuna. Note that two LCACs performed a "Side Too" landing, by turning the crafts so that they are parallel to the ocean. This allows vehicles to exit the landing craft and drive on to hard-packed sand without getting stuck. In this photo, an M-1A1 Abrams main battle tank, a Humvee, and an LAV-25 head inland as part of the assault team. *S. F. Tomajczyk*

self-sustaining for up to 15 days, the MEU consists of a reinforced infantry battalion, a composite aviation squadron (20 helicopters and 6 AV-8B Harriers), and a service support group (motor transport, military police, and landing support). The MEU is heavily armed with a variety of weapon systems, including 5 M-1A1 Abrams Main battle tanks, 8 155-millimeter howitzers, 12 amphibious assault vehicles (such as the AAVP-7), 9 60-millimeter mortars, and numerous antitank launchers.

By contrast, a Marine expeditionary force (MEF)—the largest organizational unit of a fleet Marine force—is comprised of 30,000-plus Marines (one or more divisions and an aircraft wing) under the command of a lieutenant general. It is capable of being self-sustaining for up to 60 days and has 150 helicopters, 150 aircraft, 70 tanks, 108 155-millimeter howitzers, and more.

There are always Marine units afloat in amphibious ships in forward areas. Normally, an MEU is based aboard ARGs located in the Mediterranean area and another in the Pacific/Indian Ocean region. Additional MEUs are usually in transit to relieve forward-deployed MEUs or are engaged in training exercises.

Amphibious ready groups are often assigned to and escorted by an aircraft carrier battle group, especially when the CVBG is forward deployed to an area of the world where a crisis requiring the assistance of the Marines could arise.

For instance, in June 1999, the 26th MEU/SOC (SOC stands for special operations capable) assigned to the USS *Kearsarge* (LHD-3) amphibious ready group, which was part of the USS *Enterprise* battle group, went ashore at Litokhoran, Greece, and headed through Macedonia to provide security for refugee camp construction in the war-torn Balkan region. The entire MEU was unloaded to the beach in 34 hours and established a forward operating base in Macedonia only 42 hours after the unloading began.

An aerial view of the amphibious assault ship USS *Bataan* (LHD-5) as it patrols the fictitious Gulf of Sabani during JTFEX 99-2. The largest amphibious assault ships in the world, the Wasp-class ships accommodate 1,894 Marines as well as 30 helicopters and 6 to 10 AV-8B Harrier "jump jets." In their stern well deck, they hold three LCACs. They are capable of projecting tremendous military power anywhere in the world. *S. F. Tomajczyk*

A quiet end to a busy day aboard the USS *Bataan*. Three gents chat among themselves at the ship's stern in the shadow of the AV-8B Harrier, a single-engine, vertical/short takeoff and landing (V/STOL) aircraft used by the Marine Corps for light attack and close-air support roles. It has a combat range of 165 miles carrying 12 500-pound bombs with one-hour loiter. A wide variety of pods, dispensers, fuel tanks, and weapons can be slung from the six wing pylons, including B-61 nuclear bombs. The aircraft is also armed with a five-barrel, 25-millimeter cannon with 300 rounds. *S. F. Tomajczyk*

In August 1999, the 26th MEU was called upon again, this time to assist with survivors of a tremendous earthquake in western Turkey that killed more than 15,000 people. For three weeks, the MEU distributed tents, bedding supplies, portable toilets, water, sump pumps, generators, medical supplies, and other relief equipment to the victims. They also prepared 10 tent sites in the towns of Golcuk, Halidere, Degermendere, Dogu Kisla, Korfez, and Arsenal.

In spite of the force projection represented by an ARG/MEU team, it is not adequate enough to respond to a major conflict, such as when the United States responded to Iraq's invasion of Kuwait in 1990 with Operation Desert Shield. In these instances, the MEU serves as a temporary 911 Band-Aid force until a marine expeditionary force arrives. Some military-affairs experts anticipate that in a sudden, bloody conflict—in which it takes an MEF several days or weeks to arrive on scene—the Pentagon could expect 90 percent casualty rates among its deployed MEU.

To speed the process of deploying a marine expeditionary force, and to equip it, the Navy has prepositioned 13 T-AK designated cargo ships at strategic locations around the world. Known as the Maritime Prepositioning Force (MPF), these three squadrons, each made up of four to five merchant vessels, are located at Diego Garcia, Chagos Archipelago (Indian Ocean), Guam/Saipan (Western Pacific), and in the western Mediterranean. Each squadron of ships contains weapons, vehicles, ammunition, fuel, water, and 30 days of provisions for three Marine amphibious brigades, totaling 46,000 men.

The flight deck of the USS *Bataan,* crowded with aircraft that will be used the following morning during an amphibious assault on the fictitious nation, Kartuna. In the foreground is the AH-1W Super Cobra attack helicopter, a deadly aircraft that provides air support to the assault force. The flight deck can accommodate 24 helicopters and 6 Harriers. The CH-46 Sea Knights are usually parked toward the bow ("Forward Bone"), while the CH-53 Super Stallions and AV-8B Harriers are spotted toward the stern ("Rear Bone"). In some situations, such as bad weather, all aircraft are parked in the below-deck hangar in an exercise known as Stuffex ("Max Pack"). It takes about six hours to accomplish this task, with the aircraft crammed in like sardines—just inches to spare between them. *S. F. Tomajczyk*

This is 0400 hours in the below-deck hangar of the USS *Bataan*. Hundreds of armed Marines from the 22d MEU (SOC) prepare to embark aboard the ship's three LCACs and head for the beach. The Marines are grouped by which assault wave they will be participating in. There are approximately seven waves, each tasked with transporting specific equipment. Note that although the *Bataan* is large enough to carry upward of 40 aircraft, space is at a premium, as is evident by the aircraft pods suspended from the ceiling. As for the yellow lighting, it is not a film-processing error. That's the high-contrast lighting used in the hangar area so that foreign objects and debris, which might contaminate a jet engine, are easier to spot and remove. *S. F. Tomajczyk*

Under the MPF premise, Marine forces would be airlifted by C-5 Galaxy, C-141 StarLifter, and C-17 Globemaster cargo planes directly to the area of conflict, where they would unite with maritime prepositioning ships and reinforce the MEU, if it is nearby. The Marines are expected to be combat-ready within five days.

During Operation Desert Shield, all three MPS squadrons unloaded their cargo in Saudi Arabia for use by all combat forces beginning in mid-August 1990. The MPS squadrons from Diego Garcia and Guam were the first to arrive, bringing M-60 tanks, 155 howitzers, and lightly armored vehicles and amphibian tractors.

The Princess Gator

If the aircraft carrier is the queen of the CVBG, then the amphibious assault ship is the princess of the ARG. Resembling an aircraft carrier in appearance, albeit a smaller version, the amphibious assault ship is designed to transport Marines and their combat equipment ashore using helicopters and LCACs. Its secondary role is to use AV-8B Harrier jets and anti-submarine warfare helicopters to perform sea control and limited power projection missions.

There are two types of amphibious assault ships in service with the Navy: the Tarawa-class, designated LHAs, and Wasp-class, designated LHDs. Each Tarawa-class ship displaces 39,400 tons fully loaded and is capable of carrying 1,900 Marines. It features extensive command and communications facilities, three operating rooms and 300 beds for wounded Marines, a special 5,000-square-foot room that allows Marines to exercise in a controlled environment similar to that in which they will be deployed, about 30,000 square feet of vehicle storage space, and 110,000 cubic feet of cargo storage space.

Three fully loaded LCACs patiently wait in the USS *Bataan's* well deck. In just a few moments, the stern gate will drop and the *Bataan* will sink 8 feet to allow the landing craft to back out and head for shore. Before the LCACs start their engines, side doors along the length of the well deck will be opened to vent the exhaust and to prevent the ship's hull from being overpressurized. The red lighting scheme is used to preserve the LCAC crew's night vision; the assault will begin at 0430 hours. Note the cabin ("cockpit") to the left. It houses the four-man LCAC crew. *S. F. Tomajczyk*

A SEAL delivery vehicle emerges from one of two dry-deck shelters attached to a submarine. Navy SEALs will swim out of the sub, get into the SDV, and then head toward a distant shore. SDVs are ideal vehicles for reconnaissance missions, such as those done prior to an amphibious assault. The assault force needs to know information about currents, underwater geography, obstacles, enemy positions, compactness of the beach, tides, and so on. *U.S. Navy*

The flight-deck control room aboard the USS *Nassau* (LHA-4). Just like an aircraft carrier, an amphibious assault ship must spot aircraft on its flight deck. As can be seen here, a tabletop scale model of the *Nassau* is used to show the status of all aircraft on the flight deck. In this case, two CH-46A Sea Knight helicopters are parked to the right (with their dual rotors fully open), and three AV-8B Harriers are parked to the rear right, astern the ship's island. *S. F. Tomajczyk*

The ships' stern docking well, which is 268 feet long and 78 feet wide, can accommodate the following landing craft arrangements: 4 LCU-1610s or 3 LCM-8s and 2 LCUs or 17 LCM-6s or 45 amphibious assault vehicles; generally, only one LCAC can be carried.

As for aircraft, Tarawa-class gators typically carry 24 CH-46 and CH-53 helicopters and 6 AV-8B Harrier Vertical/Short Takeoff and Landing (V/STOL) "jump jets." The ships are armed with two 5-inch guns, six 25-millimeter machine guns, and two 20-millimeter Phalanx CIWSes. Beginning in 1992, the ships were outfitted with two Rolling Airframe Missile launchers, which replaced two eight-cell Sea Sparrow missile launchers.

The new Wasp-class (LHD 1-6) amphibious assault ship began entering service in 1989. These ships, the largest amphibious ships in the world, are similar to the Tarawa-class, except that they have less vehicle and cargo storage space, carry more aircraft and LCACs, and have relocated vital command and communications facilities into the hull for better protection against enemy attack. A Wasp-class ship, which is staffed by 1,004 enlisted personnel and 104 officers, can carry 1,894 Marines, as well as 30 helicopters and 6 to 10 AV-8B Harriers.

The ships are also armed with two eight-cell NATO Sea Sparrow missile launchers, eight .50-caliber machine guns, and three 20-millimeter Phalanx CIWSes.

Landing craft exit through a stern docking well that can accommodate three LCACs.

The ships have an overall length of 844 feet and are 106 feet wide, displacing 40,500 tons fully loaded.

U.S. Navy

The Expeditionary Warfare Training Group (EWTG) is responsible for training Navy and Marine Corps personnel in how to conduct amphibious operations and maintain ready forces that can project power from the sea. To accomplish this, the Navy has two EWTGs: one assigned to the U.S. Pacific Command (Naval Air Base Coronado, California) and the other to the U.S. Atlantic Command (Naval Air Base Little Creek, Virginia). These facilities provide training in such diverse areas as shipboard engineering, naval gun fire support, seamanship, reconnaissance, logistics, LCAC, small boat operations, and small arms training.

One of the more interesting training tools is the Amphibious Demonstrator located at Little Creek. Essentially, it is a huge indoor model (measuring 96 by 69 feet) of a coastline on which a complete amphibious assault can be simulated. It uses scale models of ships, planes, helicopters, and so on, to show step-by-step how various assault tactics are played out, from initial reconnaissance operations to post-landing operations. Special sound and light effects are used to make the scenario as realistic as possible.

For instance, an electronic device simulates shore bombardment of the beach from warships stationed off the coast. When a ship fires its gun, a flash of light is emitted with a report of an explosion or shell burst on the terrain. A delay is built into the scenario to represent the actual time of flight of the projectile from ship to shore.

One-third of the Amphibious Demonstrator is taken up by the simulated terrain, which can be modified to represent an actual coastline anywhere in the world. The remaining two-thirds is dedicated to the sea area off the coast, where amphibious assault ships and naval gunfire support ships are positioned. Special lighting can mimic any portion of a day, from midnight to sunrise or sunset.

Navy SEALs climb out of an aircraft carrier to board their rigid-hull, inflatable boats (RHIB). These are ideal craft for reconnaissance missions and to insert and extract special-operations forces as part of an amphibious assault. There is a movement within the Navy to remove the SEALs from aircraft carriers, but the battle group commanders are resisting the effort. They like the capabilities and options that the SEALs provide them. SEALs stand out on an aircraft carrier since they are the only individuals permitted to be armed. They also spend a lot of time behind locked doors doing mission planning. *S. F. Tomajczyk*

Since they have a relatively flat-bottomed hull, they are infamous for their side-to-side rocking motion in heavy seas.

The Other ARG "Frogs"

A typical three-ship amphibious ready group has either an LHA or an LHD as its centerpiece. Supporting it are two other gators: an amphibious transport dock ship (LPD) and a dock landing ship (LSD).

There are three ship classes with the LSD designation: Harpers Ferry class, Whidbey Island class, and the aging (and soon to be decommissioned) Anchorage class. All are tasked with supporting amphibious operations, including the landing of Marine forces by LCAC, conventional landing craft, and helicopter (which are provided by the amphibious assault ships).

The ships of the Whidbey Island class, which displace 15,939 tons fully loaded, can carry 504 Marines and their equipment. Internally, they have 12,500 square feet of vehicle storage space and 5,000 cubic feet of cargo storage space. A huge stern docking well, the largest of any amphibious ship, accommodates 4 LCACs or 21 LCM-6s or 64 AAVP-7 amphibious assault vehicles. Additionally, a large helicopter deck astern allows the boarding of CH-53 and smaller helicopters.

The Harpers Ferry class is the newest and largest (16,708 tons full displacement) of the dock landing ships. Similar in design to the Whidbey Island class, these gators carry about 500 Marines and their equipment, but have a smaller docking well and much more cargo storage space (40,000 cubic feet as opposed to 5,000 cubic feet). Their docking well, however, can still store two LCACs.

As for dock landing ships, there is only one class in service: the Austin class (LPD 4-15). These vessels, which transport Marines for amphibious operations, displace 17,000 tons fully loaded and carry 930 Marines and their equipment. (Some ships in this class also carry a flagstaff of about 90 personnel.) They have about 12,000 square feet of vehicle storage space and 40,000 cubic feet of cargo storage space. All of these ships have a flight deck above the stern docking well with two landing spots for helicopters. The ships are capable of transporting up to six CH-46 Sea Knight helicopters for short distances. As for the docking well, it can accommodate several LCM-6 and LCM-8s or up to 28 AAVP-7 amphibious assault vehicles. Although, technically speaking, a single air-cushioned LCAC can fit inside the well, it is an *extremely* tight fit, with only a few inches of clearance on either side. For this reason, LCACs are not carried, except in dire situations, and even then only on a calm day

The USS *Whidbey Island* (LSD-41) returns to Little Creek, Virginia, at dawn after finishing her role in JTFEX 99-2. Internally, she has 12,500 square feet of storage space for tanks and combat vehicles, plus 5,000 cubic feet of space for cargo and provisions. Her rear well deck accommodates four LCAC or 64 amphibious assault vehicles. *S. F. Tomajczyk*

when there are no waves to toss the LCAC around as it embarks or debarks.

The Navy is currently building the next generation of LPDs, now known as the San Antonio class (LPD-17). These $641 million ships will displace 24,900 tons fully loaded and will be capable of carrying up to four CH-46 Sea Knights and up to two MV-22 Osprey tilt-rotor aircraft. The Marine detachment will number about 720. The first two ships of this class, the San Antonio and New Orleans, are now under construction.

Amphibious Assault!

The United States has a reputation as possessing the strongest and best-trained amphibious force in the world. Since the days of World War II when American naval expeditionary troops took control of the Pacific by pushing the Japanese back across the ocean island-by-island, every nation has admired the power that is

inherent in an amphibious assault force—and no one wants to be on the receiving end of it.

This was quite apparent during the 1991 Gulf War when Saddam Hussein and his military leaders focused their defensive efforts at preventing a U.S.-led amphibious assault against Iraqi shores by planting underwater minefields, placing obstacles thickly across the beaches, and positioning army assets toward the Persian Gulf to repel an attack. In the process, they forgot about the possibility of an end-around sweep or a rear attack. But you can't really blame them for being blind: the United States went out of its way to tease and taunt them by parading its amphibious forces throughout the Gulf. It was an act of classic deception, and the Iraqis bought it hook, line, and sinker.

Although some critics arrogantly declare that amphibious warfare is an antiquated and unneeded art, especially in a world marked by tactical missiles

A glance inside the hectic world of PriFly aboard the USS *Nassau* (LHA-4). The air boss (right) and mini boss (left) coordinate the launch and recovery of all aircraft on the flight deck. As with an aircraft carrier, they own all the airspace out to 10 miles from the ship. When a helicopter or Harrier lands aboard an amphibious assault ship, it flies up the starboard side of the ship, crosses the bow, and then approaches the designated landing spot (one of nine) from the port side. This simple procedure becomes more hazardous during stormy weather and during night operations when pilots wear night-vision goggles. *S. F. Tomajczyk*

and heavily armed, supersonic jets, naval leaders vehemently disagree. They are quick to point out that the majority of conflicts and crises occurring since World War II have taken place in the littoral regions of the world, *not* deep inside a continent where standoff weapons are required. They also highlight that the majority of the world's population centers are located within 200 miles of the coast, easily within the range of a carrier battle group and its amphibious ready group. Hence, the doctrines and tactics of amphibious warfare, obviously modified and refined since World War II, are necessary now more than ever.

So how does the United States conduct an amphibious assault? Well, that changes situation to situation, of course, but there is an accepted approach that we will explore here.

The first step, as is so common in all military operations, is to collect intelligence. Yes, a CVBG/ARG/MEU team needs to know where the enemy is positioned, how strong its forces are, and what it is doing, BUT! It also needs to know more important information. What's more important than knowing what the enemy is doing? Well, such things as the underwater typography, water depth, current strength and direction, seafloor slope, underwater obstacles, the compactness of the beach sand, shoreline obstacles, and enemy defenses, both above and below water. Remember, an amphibious assault means that Marines are being transported from ship to shore. Anything and everything about the landing area must be known to prevent landing craft from hitting a mine, running aground, or entering an enemy kill zone.

To gather this intelligence, the CVBG and ARG have several resources available to them. For instance, the battle group commander can order an F-14 Tomcat, F/A-18 Hornet, or even a UAV to do flyovers of the beach area and take photos. Doing that, however, is likely to attract unwanted attention. A more stealthy option is to send in one of the nuclear attack submarines to check things out. The drawback to doing that is the submarine could find itself in the middle of a minefield or run aground on a sandbar. Furthermore, because of its sheer size, a sub simply cannot get close enough to the beach to check everything out.

So to learn everything there is to know about the beach, the battle group commander calls on a Navy SEAL platoon or squad, or on the reconnaissance detachment from the embarked MEU to physically swim ashore and scout out the area. These elite teams use a variety of means to travel from the CVBG/ARG to the beach, including SCUBA, low-visibility combat rubber raiding rafts and electric-powered, miniature submarines known as seal-delivery vehicles (SDV). The Mark VIII and Gator-class SDVs are widely used today and can be deployed worldwide aboard surface ships and submarines.

Once the amphibious assault plan has been determined, based on the collected intelligence, the next step is to get the Marines and their combat gear quickly and safely ashore. The best way to achieve this is through the combined use of helicopters and land-

Unlike an aircraft carrier, an amphibious assault ship does not use a catapult to launch its helicopters and Harriers. This causes a dilemma since every aircraft model has different aerodynamics. Complicating matters is the fact that air does not flow uniformly over the amphibious assault ship's flight deck; swirls and eddies routinely form. What this means is that the air boss and mini boss must calculate the "wind envelope" for each aircraft *before* a launch or recovery attempt is made. They use a device called a "Whiz" to determine what direction the ship should be turned in (taking into consideration the wind and other environmental factors) to facilitate a safe launch or landing. They provide the directions to the ship's bridge by phone. *S. F. Tomajczyk*

ing craft. The undisputed King of amphibious transport is the air-cushioned LCAC. As mentioned earlier in this chapter, the amphibs usually carry one to four of these fast and powerful craft in their well docks.

The LCAC was designed to carry a 70-ton payload into a 25-knot headwind with 4- to 6-foot seas at 50 knots. It's an incredible feat of naval engineering. And since the LCAC floats about 5 feet above the ocean and land, it can gain access to 75 percent of the beaches in the world, regardless of the coastlines' ruggedness. (By comparison, conventional landing craft can land at only 15 percent of the coasts.) Almost nothing can stop this beast. Even if the containment skirt ("bag") suffers a significant tear, the LCAC can still maneuver.

Although vehicles, tanks, and amphibious vehicles are driven aboard the LCAC and chained down,

the Marines must climb inside a large, windowless, metal box container known as the Personnel and Troop Module (PTM). The PTM seats up to 150 Marines and their combat gear. Once inside, the hatch is shut and the Marines sit like sardines waiting for the LCAC to make its quick trip from the gator to the beachhead. The purpose of the PTM is to protect the Marines from the heavy sea spray kicked up by the LCAC slicing through the waves, and to prevent anyone from being tossed overboard or, worse yet, blown into the enormous propeller blades that drive the LCAC forward.

Amphibious assaults are conducted in a series of "waves." This is because a CVBG/ARG does not have enough landing craft to simultaneously land 2,200 Marines. The first wave usually consists of five or six LCACs loaded with Marines who will form the point of the invasion force. These LCACs unload from their host gators and meet up in the ocean at a "holding point," which is located 5 to 15 miles off shore. When the order is given, the LCACs speed to the coast at 40 to 50 knots.

Simultaneously, an air combat element (ACE) is launched from the amphibs to provide air cover or to travel inland to a landing zone and drop off a forward combat team that is tasked with conducting a specific mission. The ACE is usually comprised of AH-1W Super Cobra attack helicopters, CH-46 and CH-53 troop-carrying helicopters, and AV-8B Harrier jets.

As the LCACs approach the beach, they are greeted by flashlight-waving members of the beach landing party, who were inserted by aircraft or other means hours or, in some instances, days earlier. The beachmaster owns the beach and no one, not even an LCAC, can come ashore without his or her permission and guidance. When an LCAC comes ashore, it slows down to about 15 knots and zips up onto the beach; none of the Marines aboard the LCAC in the PTM feels the transition from ocean to land. The ride is that smooth.

Once ashore, the "Hopper," as the beach landing party refers to the LCAC, spins sharply 90 degrees to the right in a maneuver known as a "Side Too." This positions the bow of the LCAC so that it is parallel to the ocean. It allows the vehicles aboard to be driven off onto hard-packed sand instead of loose sand that might cause them to get stuck. As soon as the LCAC is unloaded, it reinflates its skirt, turns about, and heads back to the amphibs for the next load.

In any given amphibious assault, there are several landings made. The first two waves bring ashore Marines and their amphibious assault vehicles (such as the AAVP-7). They are followed by two more waves that transport Humvees armed with .50-caliber machine guns, lightly armored vehicles (LAV-25), M-1A1 Abrams main battle tanks, and antitank TOW missile launchers. The remaining waves (the number varies by the mission) bring ashore artillery (155-millimeter howitzers) and logistical support units. The second and later waves are usually done by a host of landing craft, not just the LCAC. The more common craft include LCMs (land craft, mechanized), LCUs (landing craft, utility), and occasionally LSTs (tank landing ships).

From start to finish, an ARG can unload an entire MEU and its combat gear within 36 hours. If speed is of the essence, CH-46 and CH-53 helicopters can be used to transport vehicles and cargo ashore, supplementing the unloading process.

If, at any time, the amphibious assault force or the forward-deployed combat team come under enemy threat or hostile fire, the naval surface warships that escorted the ARG from the rear-deployed CVBG to the shore, jump into the fray. They fire their guns and missiles at enemy positions, which are called in by Marines, the beach landing party, or aircraft flying in the area. This is known as naval gun fire support, and its sole purpose is to protect American lives while forcing the enemy to retreat.

By the time an MEU has completely unloaded from the gators, the point components of the assault force are already several miles inland. What was once a

The tilt-rotor MV-22B Osprey makes an approach to the flight deck of the USS *Saipan* (LHA-2). Scheduled to enter military service in 2002, the Osprey will be used by the Marine Corps to transport its Marines ashore from over-the-horizon during an assault. It can be up and out of a landing zone in less than half the time it takes a CH-46 Sea Knight to depart because it can accelerate from 0 to 280 miles per hour in just 63 seconds. The Osprey will allow the Marines to move inland more quickly and farther than is now possible with helicopters, forcing the enemy to spread its military assets over a larger area. *U.S. Navy*

naval conflict has metamorphosed into a land battle. From here on out, the CVBG and ARG play a supporting role to the ground pounder in the field, providing him with fire support, air cover, airlift capability, replenishment of supplies, and, if necessary, medical services aboard the amphibious assault ship.

If history is any indicator, it won't be long before the ARG is transporting the Marines back aboard, the battle or crisis having been quickly and decisively resolved.

The fast combat support ship USS *Seattle* (AOE-3) conducts an underway replenishment of the USS *Bataan* at dusk during JTFEX 99-2. For nearly an hour cargo, fuel, and provisions are sent across by cable from the Seattle. *S. F. Tomajczyk*

Chapter 8

Replenishment
Beans, Bullets, and Bandages

It's no secret: To win a war, military forces must be well supplied and well fed. Admirals and generals have known this fact for centuries. No military unit can function with empty rifles, empty gas tanks, or empty stomachs. Because of this, replenishment plays a vital role in carrier battle group operations for it dictates how responsive the warships will be when a threat arises. Hence, whenever a CVBG heads to sea, careful thought and planning is given to when, where, and how food, aviation fuel, repair supplies, and ordnance will be replenished.

Even though a nuclear carrier can steam more than a million miles before refueling, she's always limited by her onboard supply of food, aviation fuel, and ordnance. Run out of any of those and all you've got is a billion dollar paperweight.

Sailor aboard the USS *George Washington* (CVN-73)

The Navy maintains bases around the world in allied nations not only to have a presence there to maintain peace, but also to have a place where its warships can set anchor and restock their shelves and storage holds with needed supplies. For example, carrier battle groups of the Navy's Sixth Fleet, which patrol the Mediterranean Sea, routinely anchor in Naples, Italy, to take on food, fuel, mail, and reassigned personnel. It is a comfortable and expeditious arrangement. On occasion, the fleet will also stop at other ports-of-call in the Mediterranean region, such as Rota, Spain, to reinforce America's military commitment to the host nation and, you guessed it, to replenish supplies.

Unfortunately, this peaceful and convenient scheme does not work in some places of the world where the United States finds itself among decidedly unfriendly nations. The Persian Gulf is one such region.

And so, to ensure their autonomy and to ensure their ability to wage war at any given moment, American battle groups routinely head for sea accompanied by at least one replenishment ship. The most commonly used vessels are the fleet oilers (AO) and the fast combat support ship (AOE).

Cimarron-class fleet oilers (AO 177–180 and –186) carry 183,000 barrels of petroleum products. This is enough to refuel a nonnuclear-powered aircraft carrier (such as the *John F. Kennedy*) twice and up to eight escort ships once.

As for the fast combat support ships, they provide rapid transfer of petroleum, fuel, ammunition, *and* stores to the aircraft carrier and her screening surface combatants. There are presently two classes of AOE in service: the Supply class (AOE 6–9) and the Sacramento class (AOE 1–4).

The Supply class ships are the newest floating warehouses in the Navy's fleet, having entered service in 1993. Measuring 755 feet long and displacing 48,800 tons when fully loaded, they have a cargo capacity of 156,000 barrels of petroleum products plus 1,800 tons of ammunition, 400 tons of refrigerated provisions, and 250 tons of dry stores. They carry three CH-46 Sea Knight helicopters to transport goods from ship to ship. For limited protection against enemy attack, they are armed with an eight-tube NATO Sea Sparrow missile launcher, two 20-millimeter Phalanx CIWSes, and two 25-millimeter

A CH-53E Super Stallion conducts a VERTREP operation aboard the flight deck of the USS *Bataan* (LHD-5). The helicopter is strong enough to lift 16 tons of cargo slung beneath it. Based on this, the Super Stallion can lift 90 percent of the combat equipment used by a Marine division. *S. F. Tomajczyk*

cannons. Additionally, they are equipped for protection against chemical, biological, and nuclear attack.

The Sacramento-class ships, which were commissioned from 1964 to 1970, are 794 feet long and displace 53,600 tons when fully loaded. Each vessel has a cargo capacity of 156,000 barrels of petroleum products, 2,100 tons of ammunition, 250 tons of refrigerated provisions, and 250 tons of dry stores. They carry two helicopters and are armed with a NATO Sea Sparrow launcher, two Phalanx CIWSes, and four .50-caliber machine guns.

Both the Supply and Sacramento classes of ships are able to travel at speeds in excess of 25 knots. This is important since they must keep up with the CVBG when it is steaming to a crisis or armed conflict. And it is precisely during these times of imminent battle that the AOEs are needed most. For they carry the JP-5 aviation fuel that all aircraft will need, the missiles and ammo that the destroyers and cruisers will need, the bombs and rockets that the F-14s and F/A-18s will need, and the food that everyone will need to remain healthy and alert.

When deployed, the AOEs are usually positioned by the battle group commander toward the rear of the group, in an area safely away from the direction of possible threats. This is for two reasons: First, the AOEs are lightly armed, and therefore cannot engage in serious warfare against a heavily armed guided-missile destroyer. Second, the AOEs, with their tons of supplies and flammable products, present a tempting target for enemy forces to go after. Sink just one AOE and it could easily jeopardize military operations.

Since even these monstrous AOEs eventually run out of supplies during the CVBG's six-month deployment, the Navy supplements its replenishment efforts with auxiliary supply and cargo ships operated by the Military Sealift Command (MSC), which is a component of the U.S. Transportation Command. The majority of these ships are older and were designed for specific missions: ammunition ships (T-AE), fleet stores ships (T-AF), combat stores ships (T-AFS), hospital ships (T-AH), transport oilers (T-AOT), gasoline tankers (T-AOG), oilers (T-AO), and so on. They are generally operated by Merchant Marine personnel but have a small detachment of Navy personnel aboard to provide communications and to assist with helicopter operations and munitions handling.

Several of these auxiliary ships are pulled together to form what is known as an underway replenishment force. They meet up with the CVBG and provide replenishment services until either they are no longer needed or they run out of provisions. There are four underway replenishment groups assigned to the Navy's Seventh Fleet (Western Pacific and Indian Ocean), two with the Sixth Fleet (Mediterranean), three with the Second Fleet (Atlantic), and one with the Third Fleet (Eastern Pacific).

Transferring the Goods

Ship-to-ship restocking of an aircraft carrier and its protective screen of surface combatants with provisions, fuel, and ammunition can often be accomplished in sheltered water, like a bay or harbor, with both ships stationary. This, in fact, is often done with tenders servicing submarines or destroyers in times of peace or, during war, in safe, rear-area ports.

But since the purpose of a CVBG is to have a forward presence in troubled areas of the world, playing the role of the proverbial snarling watchdog, it simply cannot stop dead in the water to take on bombs and candy bars. To do so would endanger the safety of the entire battle group as it would become a huge floating target. Recall that the ability to maneuver and respond quickly to a dynamic and ever-changing situation is what allows a CVBG to dominate the battle space. Bobbing impotently up and down in the waters off the coast of a hostile nation to load provisions from a supply ship is neither a wise nor healthy thing to do.

For exactly that reason, warships of a carrier battle group routinely replenish while underway at sea. This is achieved through rigs and helicopters.

Rig transfer (also known as, "underway replenishment") is done by the supply ship coming closely alongside the carrier or surface combatant so that it perfectly matches the ship's speed and heading. A line is then shot across the 100-foot separation between the two ships, to which a 1-inch or thicker jackstay, or cable, is attached. To this cable is affixed a pulley-like "travel block" from which the netted cargo is slung.

Care is taken to ensure that the tension in the cable is kept as constant as possible. If there is too much strain, the wire will snap and the cargo will splash into the ocean. Furthermore, the recoiling wire can severely injure or kill someone on both ships. By contrast, if not enough tension is maintained, the wire will sag and the cargo will drag through the waves. This, too, can eventually cause the cable to snap.

The travel block is pulled across the jackstay from the supply ship to the carrier by either a winch or hydraulic arm. This rig setup is commonly used to move solid stores, up to 3,000 pounds per load, from ship to ship. The system is also used to move fuel lines across the space between the two ships so that oil, JP-5 aviation fuel, and so on, can be pumped.

During the replenishment process, which can last an hour or longer, the two vessels are constantly monitoring the sea conditions as well as their ship handling. Since they are vulnerable to hostile attack, particularly by aircraft and submarines in times of war, the ships zigzag by altering their course 5 or 10

While not the most attractive military aircraft, the C-2A Greyhound is arguably the busiest, transporting up to 28 passengers or 10,000 pounds of cargo to and from aircraft carriers. The aircraft, which is based on the same frame as that used by the E-2C Hawkeye, is stressed for catapult launches and arrested landings; its wings fold for carrier stowage. The Greyhound is traditionally parked on the flight deck immediately adjacent to the island so that visiting dignitaries do not get sucked into jet intakes, blown overboard, or torched by an afterburner. The C-2A shown in this photo happens to be the aircraft the author flew on out to the USS *John F. Kennedy* (CV-67). A photographer aboard the carrier snapped the photo as the plane (and author) did an "Okay Three" trap. *U.S. Navy*

degrees at a time. Changes in course are determined and controlled by the delivering ship.

To reduce the risk of being detected by electronic emissions, communication between the two ships during replenishment operations is often done through the use of lights or flag signals.

Most ships have a designated replenishment crew trained in handling the jackstays and unloading the netted cargo. Aboard aircraft carriers, these men and women are identified by their green jerseys and white cranials. During actual replenishment operations, only these individuals are permitted to be anywhere near the jackstays and cargo. Others may watch, but from a safe distance only. People have been known to be crushed by falling cargo, beheaded by snapped cables, or tossed overboard by swinging, wayward cargo nets.

Sacks and sacks of a sailor's favorite cargo—mail—are unloaded from a CH-53D Sea Stallion helicopter on the flight deck of the USS *Nimitz* (CVN-68). The carrier and its battle group were on patrol in the Persian Gulf at the time supporting Operation Southern Watch. *U.S. Navy*

Up, Up, and Away!

Helicopters are often used to restock carrier battle groups. Known in Navy parlance as vertical replenishment (VERTREP), this is a faster replenishment method since it avoids the time-consuming maneuvers of carefully positioning ships alongside each other. Additionally, a helicopter can lift more cargo per load than a rig system.

For example, the Navy's twin-rotor UH-46D Sea Knight can carry up to 3,000 pounds of cargo internally or 10,000 pounds slung from beneath its fuselage. Even more impressive is the CH-53E Super Stallion, which can carry up to 36,000 pounds of cargo underslung. This means that the Super Stallion can lift more than 90 percent of the heavy equipment in a Marine division, as compared to only about 40 percent for the CH-53D Sea Stallion, its closest competitor where cargo lift ability is concerned.

VERTREP helicopters are generally detailed to replenishment ships, such as the Mars class (AFS-1) combat stores ship, the ex-British Lyness class (T-AFS 8) combat stores ships, the Sacramento class (AOE-1)

fast combat support ships, and the Wichita class (AOR-1) replenishment oilers. Each of these ship classes has two CH-46 helicopters assigned to them. The newest, fast combat support ship, the Supply class (AOE-6), carries three helicopters.

On occasion, a warship can use its own helicopter for VERTREP purposes, but this temporarily takes away its ability to conduct antisubmarine warfare and search-and-rescue operations. Because of this, most destroyer and cruiser COs are reluctant to part with their helicopters unless it is vitally important.

In the future, the Navy's version of the unique tilt-rotor Osprey aircraft will replace the aging CH-46 Sea Knight helicopter in the VERTREP role. Able to take off and land vertically like a helicopter, and then convert into a high-speed, high-altitude turbo-prop aircraft, the Osprey has a range of 2,100 nautical miles with a single aerial refueling and can carry up to 15,000 pounds of cargo slung beneath its fuselage.

The Osprey is scheduled to begin entering military service in 2002. The Marine Corps intends to field 360 MV-22s by 2013, the Air Force to purchase 50 CV-22s (Air Force special operations variant), and the Navy to acquire 48 HV-22Bs for combat search and rescue, special warfare, and fleet logistics support.

Into the Future . . . and Beyond

The technologically advanced Osprey aside, the Navy continues to explore ways in which to support and replenish its forward-deployed warships. In today's fast-paced world, where aircraft can cross continents and oceans in hours (and missiles even less), the military no longer has the luxury of waiting days or weeks for a replenishment ship to arrive on location to resupply warships and combat troops.

One way to shorten the response time has been to preposition combat supplies aboard merchant ships anchored at various locations around the globe. Known as the Maritime Prepositioning Force (MPF), these groups of ships contain enough weapons, munitions, and a month's worth of provisions for a 16,500-man Marine expeditionary brigade. (See chapter 7.) This is great for ground combat forces (the MPF was used during the 1991 Gulf War to unload M-60 tanks, 155-millimeter howitzers, and light-armored vehicles and amphibious vehicles), but it does not necessarily help the CVBG.

Because of that, the Navy is considering a plan to link several ocean-going platforms to serve as a huge, floating logistics base. Called the Mobile Offshore Base (MOB), it would provide the theater commander with the means to mount ongoing assaults ashore without having to rely on vulnerable supply depots. It would also accommodate troops, supplies, and full-size airlifters. The platforms—each the size of an offshore oil rig—would be towed into position and then linked together in various configurations to meet the theater commander's needs. By using the MOB, the Navy would no longer be subject to restrictions by nations that host U.S. bases on their territory. And it would provide carrier battle groups with an unlimited supply source of ordnance, food, and fuel.

For inshore support, the Navy's Office of Naval Research is developing a concept for a futuristic support craft that could serve as a logistic and helicopter platform close to an enemy's coastline. Known as the littoral support craft, it is envisioned to be a high-speed, multihulled, small radar signature ship that will be capable of operating in all sea and weather conditions. Each craft (400-ton displacement) will have a large cargo volume—more than 70,000 cubic feet of space for provisions and equipment—and a large open deck from which helicopters and MV-22 Osprey tilt-rotor aircraft can operate.

Proponents of the idea are seeking $30 million from Congress to fund a demonstrator ship. If developed, the test ship could participate in the Navy's Fleet Battle Experiment program, where emerging technologies are blended with operational forces to judge their feasibility and usefulness.

The USS *Theodore Roosevelt* (CVN-71) conducts a VERTREP operation, loading bombs, missiles, and ammunition from the USS *Santa Barbara* (AE-28). The crates of ordnance are transferred from the *Barbara* to the *Roosevelt* using a CH-46 Sea Knight helicopter (from which this photo was taken). *U.S. Navy*

The guided-missile frigate USS *Ingraham* (FFG-61) receives fuel from the conventionally powered aircraft carrier USS *Kitty Hawk* (CV-63) during an underway replenishment exercise. *U.S. Navy*

Chapter 9

Preparing for War
Into Harm's Way

We live in an unsettled, bloody world. Since the end of World War II, more than 200 conflicts have been fought around the world, resulting in the deaths of more than 40 million people. In fact, at any given time, there are 40 to 100 wars being fought somewhere on the planet. Peace is a rare condition, existing only about 5 percent of the time.

> *We have an obligation to our nation and to our people to train them to be the most effective if they have to be called upon to go into combat.*
>
> Vice Admiral William Fallon,
> Commander, U.S. Second Fleet

warships, aircraft, and submarines so powerful is not just the technology behind their weapon systems but, rather, the person in uniform. It takes upward of 15,000 sailors, Marines, and aircrews to make a battle group function smoothly and effortlessly. These are dedicated men and women who are willing to work long, hard hours to ensure that the rest of us can sleep well at night.

Because of the prevalence of war and because the United States is called upon to ensure peace overseas, it is only appropriate that its military forces train daily to go into harm's way. Doing so ensures that brave, young men and women will return safely home to their loved ones after fulfilling America's commitments abroad.

Indeed, a strong-looking military force is arguably the most powerful tool in diplomacy. It backs up international agreements and trade negotiations, protects transportation routes and other economic assets, and indirectly twists the arms of resistant parties into complying with the desires of political leaders. If war breaks out, it is because a nation's military has failed to appear to be too strong to attack.

As this book has shown, the aircraft carrier battle group is the world's most powerful fighting force. When it steams off the coast of a hostile nation, it sends a clear and loud message to everyone ashore: BACKOFF! What makes this collection of

To this end, the carrier battle group never ceases to prepare for deployment. From the moment it returns from a six-month cruise overseas, it is already beginning its 18-month-long "fleeting up" preparation ritual. As mentioned in chapter 1, this process begins in earnest during the 12 months leading up to deployment. This period is marked with surface ships completing repairs, as well as making modifications or upgrades to their combat and navigation systems. Those that do acquire new equipment travel to one of several fleet operational readiness accuracy check sites (FORACS), which are located at sea off of Hawaii, southern California, and Andros Island in the Bahamas.

The Bahamas FORACS site, which is used by the U.S. Atlantic Fleet and several NATO nations, occupies a 5-by-5-mile area at sea that is filled with sensitive equipment to measure the accuracy of combat and navigation sensors found aboard ships, submarines, and helicopters. Such sensors typically

The destroyer USS *Stump* (DD-978) undergoes repairs and modifications at the Norfolk Naval Base in Virginia after returning home from a six-month-long deployment overseas. *S. F. Tomajczyk*

A look at "Carrier Row" in Norfolk, Virginia, from PriFly aboard the amphibious assault ship USS *Nassau* (LHA-4). The nearest carrier is the USS *Dwight D. Eisenhower* (CVN-69), a Nimitz-class carrier that served with distinction in the 1991 Gulf War. The other carrier in the distance is the "Big E" USS *Enterprise* (CVN-65); it was the world's second nuclear-powered warship when it was launched in 1960. In 1990, the *Enterprise* underwent a 36-month refueling and overhaul at Newport News Shipbuilding. *S. F. Tomajczyk*

include sonar, search radar, periscopes, fire control systems, and gyrocompasses. The data is transmitted to the FORACS control room ashore for analysis. If everything checks out, the ship or aircraft is given the "thumbs up."

In addition to FORACS, the Andros Island test area, the Atlantic Undersea Test and Evaluation Center, also has a weapons test range and an acoustic measurement range. The weapons range occupies a deep-water area 5 miles wide and 35 miles long. It provides 3-D tracking of antisubmarine missiles and torpedoes above (up to 70,000 feet), on, and below the water.

As for the acoustics range, it occupies a 5-by-15-mile area and is used to detect, record, and analyze hydroacoustic noise made by surface ships and submersibles, such as submarines and SEAL Delivery Vehicles (SDV). The range is especially suitable for measuring acoustic noise because of its location in a stable, quiet body of water that is 6,000 feet deep and shielded from commercial ship traffic.

In addition to finishing repairs and outfittings, the 12-month period leading up to a CVBG's deployment is also marked with numerous training exercises that are done to strengthen a variety of naval-combat skills, such as gunnery practice, electronic warfare, air intercept drills, and missile launches.

For antisubmarine warfare training, the warships and ASW aircraft head for the open ocean, where they practice against U.S. and allied attack submarines. For aerial combat, fighters duel it out in the skies over military reservations around the country. Some pilots even undergo advanced dogfight training at the Naval Strike and Air Warfare Center in Fallon, Nevada. As for anti-air warfare, both warships and fighter/strike aircraft practice shooting-down drones.

Ensign Nolo, I Presume?

Drones are remotely piloted missiles or full-scale aircraft that mimic an enemy threat, such as a speeding cruise missile or fighter. These drones are routinely used during training exercises so that Tomcats, Hornets, and surface warships can hone their combat skills and test their weapon systems.

Although drones can be taken along with a CVBG to allow its escorts and air wing to spontaneously practice warfare maneuvers while underway at sea, the drones are also flown out of test ranges in the United States. One of the best-known drone-training ranges is assigned to the Pacific Missile Test Center based at NAS Point Mugu in California. The test range encompasses a fully instrumented 35,000-square-mile area of ocean, which measures 125 miles wide and 250 miles long. It is here that a drone is sent by its operator into a waiting pack of warships or fighters, who have orders to engage it. They splash the drone with either live fire or, more frequently, with electronic sensors.

The F-14 Tomcat, for instance, is equipped with an AIM-7 Sparrow telemetry round that allows the pilot and RIO to achieve lock-on and theoretical

Sunrise finds a sailor painting the hull of the guided-missile cruiser USS *Cape St. George* (CG-71). Chippin' and paintin' is the bane of many sailors, but it is a necessary task to extend the life of the ship and to ensure her seaworthiness. *S. F. Tomajczyk*

Right: There's nothing more happy in a sailor's life than when he or she returns home after a six-month deployment overseas. The celebration starts with a hug and kiss, and ends up at the nearest fast-food restaurant, like McDonald's. *S. F. Tomajczyk*

launch of the missile without destroying the $450,000 drone. To make life more challenging for the Tomcat, the drone can be outfitted with an electronic jammer that will render the F-14's radar useless, forcing the aircrew to engage in a *mano-a-mano* dogfight with the drone. An assignment easier said than done. . . .

The Navy maintains a plethora of drones for training purposes, including those listed below:

BQM-34 Firebee—A high subsonic, sweptwing missile launched from the air or ground and controlled by a pilot using remote instruments and a computer. With its powerful engine, the Firebee is capable of high climb rates and 6-G maneuverability. Several versions of the Firebee are in the Navy's drone arsenal: The 34E is a high-altitude supersonic variant that simulates enemy aircraft. The 34S can be tailored to simulate a cruise missile or a small fighter in various threat environments. The 34T is a supersonic variant that can perform evasive maneuvers at up to 5 Gs. Firebees (and other drones) are usually launched from a DC-130A Hercules, which can carry four drones on underwing racks. Once the

Herk reaches the drop point, the drone is released and an onboard control fires up the drone's turbojet engine and begins to remotely fly it toward the contact. Carrying 600 pounds of fuel, the Firebee can fly for about 30 minutes, after which, it deploys a parachute and splashes into the ocean where it is recovered by a helicopter.

BQM-74C—A drone that simulates a sea-skimming cruise missile. It can be programmed to emit active radar signals, or it can be totally quiet. The drone is often launched at warships working up after refit or undergoing postcommissioning shakedown exercises to test its defenses against an antiship missile. On rare occasion, the ship's fire control team is allowed to launch a Standard missile at the drone, or shoot it down using the 20-millimeter Phalanx CIWS. Generally, though, the drone is splashed synthetically through computer simulation.

MQM-8G—A missile target that is capable of achieving speeds of Mach 2.8 and heights of 70,000 feet. It can also perform vertical dive attacks at up to 90 degrees against surface targets.

An SH-60B Seahawk helicopter from HSL 47 launches an AGM-119 Penguin antiship missile at an old Knox-class target ship during the Pacific naval exercise known as RIMPAC. The missile struck the ship just 24 inches above the waterline, causing severe damage. *U.S. Navy*

A NATO Sea Sparrow surface-to-air missile launches from the USS *John C. Stennis* (CVN-74) to intercept an incoming drone during a live-missile firing exercise. *U.S. Navy*

QF-4N Phantom II—A retired Phantom jet fighter that has been equipped to be flown by a pilot on the ground using remote controls. (The pilot is often referred to as *Ensign Nolo,* which stands for "No live operator.") Antennas are mounted on the aircraft's fin and wingtips to record theoretical cannon and missile shots fired by F-14 and F/A-18 aircraft. Real-time images from the Phantom's cockpit are sent to the controller pilot, along with telemetry data. All QF-4N drones are based on San Nicholas Island, a small, rocky outcrop 60 miles from Point Mugu. It has a 10,000-foot runway and an extensive collection of advanced missile-tracking and drone radio-control equipment.

Live Fire

A drone can only do so much to prepare a battle group for deployment. At some point, all the components of the CVBG have to be integrated so they function as they will in a combat situation. This is where the U.S. Atlantic Command—USACOM or ACOM for short—and joint-service training enter the picture. ACOM essentially "owns" every Army, Navy, Air Force, and Marine Corps unit based in the continental United States. It is responsible for organizing and training these units and then packaging them into a military force that can be used by the commander-in-chief of a regional command to respond to a crisis somewhere in the world. (Note: There are five regional commands, each overseeing a portion of the globe.)

This means that when America responds to a conflict or goes to war, a carrier battle group does not operate independently of other military units. When it is forward deployed, for instance, Air Force tankers may refuel its air wing while Marine EA-6B Prowlers assist in jamming enemy radar sites as Navy F-14 Tomcats escort Army C-130 Hercules that are conducting an airdrop of food and supplies.

In this joint-warfare environment, the CVBG must learn how to work with the assets of not only other military branches, but also of allied nations such as Great Britain, Canada, and Germany. This is why ACOM organizes and conducts a number of joint field-training exercises every year. Although the majority of them are moderate-sized, involving several military units in a local area, the remainder are huge: They encompass enormous tracts of land and ocean and involve dozens of ships, hundreds of aircraft, and tens of thousands of military personnel.

For example, Exercise Tandem Thrust, designed to train U.S. and Australian staffs in crisis action planning and contingency response, usually involves 28,000 personnel, 252 aircraft, and 43 ships. Larger yet is the multinational joint exercise RIMPAC, which is designed to improve the coordination of and interoperability of military forces from the U.S., Australia, Canada, Chile, Japan, and the Republic of Korea.

One of the largest exercises is the 12-day Ulchi Focus Lens, which involves nearly 20,000 U.S. sol-

The destroyer USS *Cushing* (DD-985) launches a RIM-7 Sea Sparrow surface-to-air missile from its stern mount during an exercise that took place near Kauai, Hawaii. The missile successfully intercepted a drone that had been launched from the nearby Barking Sands missile range. *U.S. Navy*

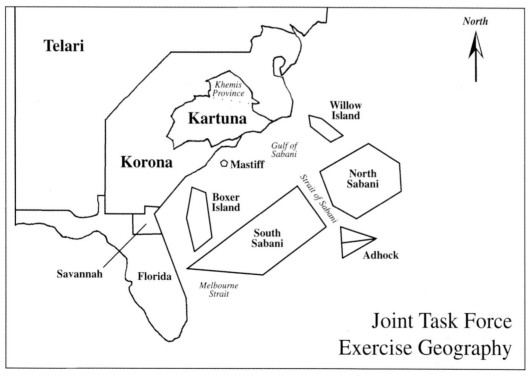

Joint Task Force Exercise Geography *S. F. Tomajczyk*

Not everything the military does is related to war. Often it is involved in humanitarian missions. The United States sent the USS *Kearsarge* (LHD-3) amphibious ready group and the 26th MEU (SOC) to Turkey after that nation suffered a devastating earthquake in August 1999. The ARG assisted victims as part of Operation Avid Response. In this photo, an LCAC prepares to enter the well deck of the USS *Gunston Hall* (LSD-44) as the ship lies at anchor in the Gulf of Izmit. The LCAC is shuttling vehicles and supplies for use by Marines and sailors ashore at Hersek, Turkey. *U.S. Navy*

diers, airmen, sailors, and Marines, along with 56,000 South Korean troops. The purpose of this annual event is to train senior officers for battle on the Korean peninsula. The USS *Blue Ridge* (LCC-19), flagship of the U.S. Seventh Fleet based in Yokosuka, Japan, serves as the command post of the exercise.

A carrier battle group, it generally participates in four or five exercises during the final six months leading up to its deployment overseas. Of these, three are considered to be vital.

The first involves the carrier's air wing. All of the squadrons that make up the air wing fly out to the Naval Strike and Air Warfare Center in Nevada for four weeks of advanced training. While at NAS Fallon, they hone their skills at the art of composite warfare and participate in a number of day and night strike missions against thousands of targets located on the 100,000-acre training facility. Their efforts are often hindered by an adversary squadron called the Desert Bogies. The "DBs" and ground units do everything in their power to prevent the air wing CAPs and Strike Teams from successfully completing their assigned missions.

The training culminates with a three-day-long exercise that requires the air wing to successfully execute a Navy-only campaign in an enemy country. In the scenario, the aircraft carrier is the first to arrive at the war zone. The air wing is tasked with holding down the fort for the first 72 hours of the war, which includes attacking key targets and conducting reconnaissance.

Needless to say, it is an intense and demanding experience that mimics the stress of actual combat. By the time it's all over, the air wing has metamorphosed from a collection of aircraft into a lethal and integrated fighting unit. Now it is ready to return to the battle group in preparation for overseas deployment.

This brings us to the two-week-long capabilities exercise (CAPEX), which is intended to blend the air wing into the battle group's operations. For the first several days, the air wing undergoes carquals followed by a number of day and night drills to demonstrate its ability to conduct reconnaissance, air combat, and strike missions.

While this goes on, the rest of the battle group is busy practicing various combat-related skills, such as battle stations, firefighting drills, ASW operations, combat search-and-rescue, electronic warfare, SIGINT collection and analysis, missile launches, ship formations, CIC drills, and gun fire support. There is often no rhyme or reason as to why one drill follows or precedes another, except that it keeps everyone tired, edgy, and off-guard. This is intentional. The battle group commander is seeking to uncover weaknesses in the battle group's ability to function. Better to identify and fix a problem now than when on patrol in enemy waters.

Depending on the combat scenarios being played out, components of the battle group—ships, submarines, and aircraft alike—often find themselves firing their guns and launching real missiles at "enemy" targets. These live-fire exercises are often done at Vieques Island (located near Puerto Rico) and San Clemente Island (located 70 miles northwest of San Diego). The islands permit large-scale invasion forces to practice live-fire, full-force amphibious assaults, naval bombardment, and combat air strikes.

On Vieques Island, for instance, Marines going ashore on "Yellow Beach" (one of three color-coded assault beaches) can call-in air strikes and naval gun-fire on targets a mile to the east. Electronic sensors positioned in the live-fire ranges judge the accuracy of weapons fire against the targets, allegedly to the nearest foot.

As for the San Clemente Island Naval Training Complex, it plays a crucial role in preparing the Navy's Pacific Fleet for combat: Destroyers pound the island's Shore Bombardment Area with their 5-inch guns, F/A-18 Hornets with their bombs. Additionally, Marines assault the beaches under the protective cover of close-air support, mine sweepers search for mines laid by warships, frigates blast inflatable "tomato" targets with their guns, helicopters launch Penguin and Harpoon antiship missiles at old Knox-class target ships, SEALs practice beach reconnaissance missions and blowing up obstacles, and submarines launch torpedoes and fire their Tomahawk land-attack cruise missiles.

Through the realistic training environments provided by Vieques and San Clemente islands, a carrier battle group is able to truly hone its combat skills, while integrating all of its components into a single, powerful military force.

Final Scrimmage: JTFEX

The last exercise a battle group undergoes is the joint task force exercise (JTFEX). It follows the joint training exercise by roughly two months and involves all assets of a CVBG, plus its ARG/MEU partner. Other military forces are involved as well, Air Force and Army units, making JTFEX the most combat-realistic training provided anywhere. The two- to three-week-long exercise takes place off the coasts of Virginia and North

Marines of the 11th MEU race through the sands of Kauai, Hawaii, to establish a strategic position following an amphibious landing in an AAVP (rear). The exercise was part of RIMPAC '96, which involved more than 44 ships, 200 aircraft, and 30,000 American military personnel. Australia, Canada, Chile, Japan, and the Republic of Korea also participated. *U.S. Navy*

Carolina and typically involve more than 15,000 personnel.

There are three interesting things about JTFEX that distinguish it from older, more-traditional war games. First, the scenario involves several fictitious nations (Korona, Kartuna, Sabani, Florida, and Telari) that are in the midst of a crisis and heightened tensions, but are not yet at war with each other. This means that the CVBG has to be diplomatic and avoid flaming the sparks into a conflagration with its presence.

Second, the exercise involves synthetic terrain. In other words, the land and ocean features that the CVBG, ARG, MEU, and Air Wing are subject to and constrained by do not really exist, except on computers and navigation charts.

And last, the JTFEX scenario lacks a highly structured schedule. This makes it a more real-world experience, introducing a sense of uncertainty as to what will transpire next. It keeps the CVBG off-guard and on its toes.

The July 1999 JTFEX (designated as JTFEX 99-2 to show that it was the second such exercise of the year) featured the USS *John F. Kennedy* Battle Group

Personnel and aircraft assigned to Carrier Air Wing 1 leave ghostly shadows and streaks of light as they move across the flight deck of the USS *George Washington* (CVN-73). They are preparing for a night of flight operations as the carrier battle group heads toward the Persian Gulf in November 1997 to join the USS *Nimitz* (CVN-68) battle group already on station. *U.S. Navy*

and the USS *Bataan* amphibious ready group, along with the 22d Marine Expeditionary Unit (Special Operations Capable) and elements of the Air Force and Army (including special operations forces).

Organizationally speaking, the JTFEX was drafted by Major General Berndt at USACOM, approved by Admiral Harold W. Gehman Jr., commander-in-chief of USACOM, and carried out by Vice Admiral William J. Fallon, who is the commander of the Second Fleet. During the exercise, Fallon assumed the role of commander of Joint Task Force 950, which embraced not only the carrier battle group, but also all the Air Force, Army, Marine, and special operations units that participated. There were 17,225 personnel involved in JTFEX 99-2, including 3,000 who served in the role of hostile, enemy forces.

In charge of all the naval forces during the exercise was Rear Admiral John M. "Carlos" Johnson who wisely elected to use the guided-missile cruiser USS *Monterey* (CG-61) as his flagship instead of the USS *Kennedy*. (It is much quieter aboard the *Monterey*. Staterooms aboard the *Kennedy* are directly below the flight deck.) Under Johnson's command and control were the Kennedy Battle Group ("Carrier Group Six"), the Bataan amphibious ready group, a patrol and reconnaissance wing, a component of Naval Special Warfare Group Two, an underway replenishment group, and the Marine's 22d MEU (SOC). The CVBG itself was comprised of the air wing (seventy aircraft), eight surface combatants, and two nuclear attack submarines.

In other words, the naval force was huge, and it was only one of several military forces that participated in JTFEX 99-2. The Air Force, for instance, contributed four B-1 and four B-52 bombers, plus a slew of F-15 Eagle fighters and several KC-135 refuelers.

The JTFEX scenario involved rising tensions between two neighboring, fictitious countries, Korona (bad guys) and Kartuna (good guys). In 1958, Kartuna declared its independence from Korona and established itself as its own nation. For the past 40-plus years, Korona has disputed the boundaries. (Note: The Navy has a detailed history of both nations in its JTFEX files, including socio-political analyses, economic data, and demographic information. Yes, the Navy takes its training scenarios *very* seriously.)

In the months prior to JTFEX 99-2, there had been increased hostility toward Kartuna by Korona, who wanted to invade its neighbor and take over rich oil fields that had been discovered. Tensions heightened further as Korona began sponsoring terrorist attacks in Kartuna, including several assassination attempts of government leaders.

The breaking point for the United Nations was when Korona mobilized its military forces and deployed them on the Kartunan border. The United Nations called for restraint and asked the United States to participate in a joint, multiforce peacekeeping mission. America obliged by ordering the USS *Kennedy* Battle Group to the Gulf of Sabani.

Upon its arrival, the battle group began conducting maritime surveillance and set up a blockade to halt suspicious ships that might be supplying potential terrorist sites in Korona with food and weapons. (Intelligence sources said that Florida was supplying Korona with weapons of mass destruction, including chemical and biological weapons.) It also began to enforce a no-fly zone over Kartuna, promising to respond to any Koronan aggression with overwhelming force.

It was during this initial three-day period that Navy leaders—anticipating the distinct possibility that an amphibious assault might be called for—ordered two SEAL platoons to begin conducting hydrographic reconnaissance of the coastline so that an assault plan could be devised. The SEALs had at their disposal two Cyclone-class coastal-patrol ships, a Rigid-Hull Inflatable Boat (RHIB) detachment that was embarked on the USS *Bataan,* and an Mk-V detachment. (Note: The Mk-V is a high-performance, 82-foot, 4,500 horsepower military jet boat that is deployable by ship or aircraft anywhere in the world within 48 hours of notification.)

Additionally, mine sweepers were ordered into the Gulf of Sabani to search for floating and bottom-anchored mines. This would clear the way for an amphibious assault force, if required. (And, of course, it was.)

As anticipated, Korona didn't take the United Nations Coalition Force very seriously and invaded Kartuna from the northwest. At the same time, Koronan-backed insurgents took control of key Kartunan facilities in the southwest region of the country.

The carrier battle group responded not only with strike missions that attacked the invading Koronan force (special operations forces assisted with the forward air control and with the lasing of targets for guided weapons), but also with an amphibious assault. Landing on the coast of Kartuna before dawn

A drone launches off the USS *Gosport's* weather deck. Used to simulate enemy aircraft attacks, the drone will fly high over the Atlantic Ocean where it will be intercepted by a surface-to-air missile launched by the USS *O'Kane* (DDG-77). *U.S. Navy*

by LCAC and other landing craft, the 2,200 Marines of the 22d MEU (SOC) quickly moved inland to fight the insurgents, take control of key facilities, and protect the U.S. Embassy. They were supported by close-air support from the carrier's air wing, as well as by naval gunfire.

The battle group itself came under attack by missiles, gunfire, and torpedoes launched by the Koronan navy. Five sailors of the USS *Seattle* (AOE-3) were injured when the oiler was struck late one evening by a surface-to-surface missile launched from a Koronan guided-missile frigate. And aboard the USS *McFaul* (DDG-74), six sailors were killed and 20 injured when it was hit by a torpedo. Additionally, the USS *The Sullivans* (DDG-68) was hit by a missile and the carrier's air wing lost one of its S-3 Viking ASW aircraft.

As is evident by the following press release sent out by the USS *Kennedy,* the fighting was intense:

Bon voyage! The USS *George Washington* (CVN-73) heads overseas for a six-month-long deployment. For families and friends left behind, this is a moment of contrasting emotions: patriotism and sadness. Tugs help guide the 97,000-ton warship safely away from the pier and out into the deeper-water shipping lanes. *U.S. Navy*

DATE: July 24, 1999
FOR IMMEDIATE RELEASE
ABOARD USS *JOHN F. KENNEDY* AT SEA—

The John F. Kennedy Battle Group, as part of joint coalition forces, continues to eliminate Koronan air, surface, and submarine forces with intense, overwhelming air and surface strikes.

The battle group, with its air wing, multiple Arleigh Burke– and Spruance-class destroyers, frigates, and guided-missile cruiser, has eliminated the majority of Koronan surface and submarine forces, including four ships, three submarines, and 24 aircraft. The Kennedy battle group will continue executing 24-hour strike missions, supporting United Nations' effort to restore peace to Kartuna.

After several days of strike missions and surface engagements, the battle group has lost one S-3 Viking aircraft, while USS McFaul and USS The Sullivans were struck by a torpedo and missile, respectively. Both ships remain fully mission capable.

As a result of the Kennedy Battle Group's immediate and lethal response to the crisis—which involved launching aircraft on combat missions 24 hours a day, in addition to coordinating naval gunfire support and air combat support for the Marines—Korona backed down on July 25 and a resolution between Kartuna and Korona was reached.

Heading Overseas

Upon the completion of JTFEX, a rating is given to the CVBG that indicates its readiness for combat. There are four readiness levels: C1 (fully combat ready), C2 (substantially combat ready), C3 (marginally combat ready; nondeployable), and C4 (not combat ready; nondeployable). The C rating system considers the condition of the equipment being used, personnel training, and the quantity and quality of equipment and supplies on hand.

If the battle group receives a C2 or higher, it will be heading to sea within six weeks after the completion of the JTFEX—just enough time to replenish the food, fuel, and ammunition used during the exercise, to make any last-minute repairs, and to allow the crew to say farewell to their families.

On the East Coast (U.S. Atlantic Fleet), the aircraft carrier heads to sea from Norfolk, Virginia, where it meets up with its escort of destroyers, cruisers, frigates, and attack submarines, which come from naval bases up and down the seaboard. A day later, the carrier's air wing flies aboard and the pilots quickly go through one last carqual session.

While this is going on, the ARG gators travel to Morehead City, North Carolina, where they pick up the Marine Corps MAGTF—usually an MEU (SOC)—from Camp Lejeune. Once the Marine contingent is aboard, the ARG heads for the open ocean to eventually meet up with the CVBG. Depending on the world situation at the time, the battle group either heads immediately to the scene of the crisis (if ordered to do so) or to the Mediterranean Sea, where it replaces the battle group that has been operating in those waters for six months and is now returning home.

And the cycle starts all over again. . . .

The Twenty-first Century Battle Group

As can be sensed from reading this book, the U.S. Navy is in the midst of tremendous change as it finds itself moving from a deep-water force that anticipated global nuclear war to a shallow-water force that must contend with low-intensity conflicts and policing actions that may involve theater missiles and weapons of mass destruction. Many of the warship classes that we once were so familiar with—Knox, Kidd, Farragut, Forrestal—have been decommissioned. The same holds true for aircraft, the most notable examples being the A-6 Intruder, ES-3A Shadow, and A-7 Corsair. Even the F-14 Tomcat is on its way out.

What we are witness to is the development of a smaller, more lethal naval force that relies on stealth technology and advanced weapon systems to do its job. The aircraft carrier battle group of the 21st century will be characterized by the following attributes:

• Real-time transfer of information from one ship or aircraft to another, using CEC to engage enemy forces in an expeditious and cost-effective manner.

• The ability to strike the enemy at farther distances and with greater accuracy using weapons that rely on GPS/INS guidance systems and computer technology. Examples include the Joint Direct Attack Munition (JDAM) and the Tactical Tomahawk.

• Enhanced intelligence collection capability as a result of using more sophisticated SIGINT, PHOTINT, and COMINT systems that will be mounted on satellites and unmanned aerial vehicles, such as Global Hawk.

• Increased firepower due to development in weapon systems, such as the Advanced Gun System and the Tactical Tomahawk.

• The introduction of expendable, unmanned aircraft to perform ultradangerous missions. This project, just now underway, refers to Unmanned Aerial Combat Vehicles (UACV) that will carry a variety of weapons.

• Fewer specialized types of aircraft within the carrier air wing. Replacing the current six distinct aircraft will be just two major designs: the Joint Strike Fighter and the Common Support Aircraft.

• Surface combatants will become technologically smarter, requiring smaller crews to staff them.

• There will be a greater reliance on stealth technology to improve the survivability of a warship by making it less detectable to the enemy. This trend is already apparent in the tentative designs for the DD-21 Land-Attack Destroyer, the Street Fighter littoral craft, and the next generation of aircraft carriers, the CVX.

• And last, there will continue to be greater integration of naval forces with other military services, until it becomes a true, blended fighting force.

Regardless of the changes that are going on, the carrier battle group will continue to serve as America's ultimate combat tool. When an aircraft carrier and its escorts suddenly show up off the coast of a nation, it will always signal America's determination to enforce its commitments and preserve peace in the world.

Baffles: The area immediately astern of a ship or submarine where it is difficult to use sonar because of the noise produced by the vessel's propeller(s). Submarines often place themselves in the baffles of an enemy ship or sub so they cannot be detected easily. A torpedo launched at the stern of a ship is known as an "up the kilt" shot.

Bag: The nickname for the inflatable skirt found on an LCAC.

Bat turn: Pilot slang for an extremely sharp turn or bank.

BB Stacker: The nickname for an ordnance man (or "ordie") aboard a carrier.

Bird farm: The nickname for an aircraft carrier.

Blue Tile Country: The central command and control area of a warship (the combat information center). So called because the deck's usual gray tiling changes to bright blue.

Bolter: On a carrier, when a landing aircraft misses all four of the arresting wires and is forced to throttle up and make another landing attempt.

Bomb farm: The stockpile of bombs, weapons, and ammunition aboard an aircraft carrier, used to rearm aircraft. "Red shirts" are responsible for maintaining the bomb farm and rearming aircraft.

CIC: The combat information center, the heart of a warship, since it is the central location where all tactical information is analyzed and displayed. The CIC is now being renamed the Combat Display Center and the Combat Direction Center (CDC).

COD: Carrier On-board Delivery, a cargo aircraft that delivers personnel, mail, and supplies to a carrier at sea. The C-2A Greyhound is the Navy's designated COD aircraft. COD is often used as a verb: "We're going to COD out at 1300 hours."

Cranial: Nickname for the protective helmet worn by the crew on the flight deck of an aircraft carrier.

Dirty Shirt: Aboard an aircraft carrier, the air wing's officer wardroom. It is the only wardroom aboard the carrier where flight suits and flight deck work gear are acceptable attire. The Dirty Shirt embraces a more informal atmosphere.

EMCON: Emissions control, the ability to control a ship's electromagnetic emissions. The greater the EMCON, the less "visible" a ship becomes to enemy sensors.

Fleet marine force: The land assault component of a naval expeditionary force. There are two fleet marine forces: one assigned to the U.S. Atlantic Command and the other to the U.S. Pacific Command. Each FMF has three divisions and three wings.

Float coat: Nickname for the vest worn by the crew on the flight deck of an aircraft carrier. The vest, which ensures a sailor's survival in case he falls overboard, contains an inflatable collar, signal beacon, sea dye marker, and a whistle. Float coats are also worn by personnel flying to and from a carrier via a COD.

Football: Nickname for the housing atop the EA-6B Prowler's tailfin that contains antenna receivers.

Frog: Nickname for members of the catapult and arresting crew because of the green-colored identifying vest they wear, and because they are always seen crouching underneath an aircraft.

Gator: Slang for an amphibious ship.

Go Fast: In antisurface warfare, jargon for a vessel moving at more than 20 knots.

Grapes: Nickname for an aircraft refueling crew member because of the purple-colored identifying vest they wear.

Hangar flying: A lively conversation among combat pilots as they recall, describe, and compare—in great detail—some of their combat flight encounters and missions.

Hangar queen: Pilot slang for an aircraft that never seems to get out of the hangar, either because it is in need of repair or because it is habitually scavenged for spare parts for other aircraft.

Hopper: Nickname beachmasters use for the LCAC.

JTFEX: Joint task force exercise, the last at-sea training a battle group undergoes prior to actual deployment.

LSO: Landing signals officer, a qualified pilot who directs aircraft of his squadron safely aboard a carrier. He has the power to wave off any aircraft he feels will not make a safe landing.

Mule: The nickname for the tow tractors used to position and jumpstart aircraft on the deck of an aircraft carrier.

NAB: Naval amphibious base.

NAS: New attack submarine, now known as the Virginia Class (SSN-774).

Knee knocker: Aboard all surface ships, this is the nickname for the steel thresholds you step over when walking down a passageway. If you don't step high enough to clear it, you'll bang your shins.

Nugget: The nickname for a rookie aviator.

Pickle: (1) The nickname for a bomb, after its pickle-like shape. (2) The nickname for the handheld control device used by the LSO.

Pig: The nickname for the firefighting tractors found aboard aircraft carriers and amphibious assault ships.

Red Bomb: The nickname for a strong sleeping pill used by pilots and aircrew who are too high strung to sleep after returning from a combat mission.

Redcrown: The codename for the ship in a CVBG that is responsible for coordinating the group's air defense efforts. The Redcrown ship, often a cruiser, is usually positioned closest to the aircraft carrier.

Redout: The reddening of a pilot's visual field caused by blood forced into his head when he experiences a negative force of gravity.

Side Too: A maneuver an LCAC makes when landing on the beach. The craft turns abruptly to the left or right so that it is parallel to the ocean. This allows vehicles to drive off the LCAC onto the hard-packed beach.

Skunk hunt (chumming): A combat tactic used by aircraft to find and destroy enemy ground targets. One aircraft flies low and slow over an area to draw enemy gunfire. When this occurs, a strike aircraft—which has been flying out of sight at higher altitude—swoops in and destroys the target with missiles and bombs.

SLCM: Submarine-launched cruise missile. Pronounced "slick-um."

Spaghetti: Pilot slang that refers to the line drawings representing an air combat maneuver.

Speed of heat: Phrase used by aircraft crew to mean "fast." The fastest level of speed is referred to as "Speed of Thought," or "Warp One."

Tonka (Tilly): Nickname for the crane found aboard aircraft carriers and amphibious assault ships (LHA, LHD) that is used to remove burning aircraft or unstable ordnance from the flight deck and dump it into the ocean. So named because of its bright yellow color, just like a child's Tonka toy. It is also sometimes referred to as "Tilly."

UNREP: Underway replenishment, the resupplying and refueling of ships at sea. The replenishment ship pulls alongside the target ship and, using strung cables, sends across provisions and fuel lines.

VERTREP: Vertical replenishment, the resupplying of ships at sea using helicopters. The provisions are slung beneath the helicopter in a special cargo net.

Index